EXPLORE
PSHE
KS4

Series Editor:
Catherine Kirk

Philip Ashton
Stephen De Silva
Lesley de Meza

DYNAMIC
LEARNING

HODDER
EDUCATION
AN HACHETTE UK COMPANY

Every effort has been made to trace all copyright holders, but if any have been inadvertently overlooked, the Publishers will be pleased to make the necessary arrangements at the first opportunity.

Although every effort has been made to ensure that website addresses are correct at time of going to press, Hodder Education cannot be held responsible for the content of any website mentioned in this book. It is sometimes possible to find a relocated web page by typing in the address of the home page for a website in the URL window of your browser.

Hachette UK's policy is to use papers that are natural, renewable and recyclable products and made from wood grown in well-managed forests and other controlled sources. The logging and manufacturing processes are expected to conform to the environmental regulations of the country of origin.

Orders: please contact Bookpoint Ltd, 130 Park Drive, Milton Park, Abingdon, Oxon OX14 4SE. Telephone: +44 (0)1235 827827. Fax: +44 (0)1235 400401. Email education@bookpoint.co.uk Lines are open from 9 a.m. to 5 p.m., Monday to Saturday, with a 24-hour message answering service. You can also order through our website: www.hoddereducation.co.uk

ISBN: 978 1 5104 7041 5

© Philip Ashton, Stephen De Silva and Lesley de Meza 2020

First published in 2020

This edition published in 2020 by

Hodder Education,

An Hachette UK Company

Carmelite House

50 Victoria Embankment

London EC4Y 0DZ

Impression number   10 9 8 7 6 5 4 3 2

Year   2024 2023 2022 2021 2020

Cover photo © rizal999 – stock.adobe.com; © melosine1302 – stock.adobe.com; © Richard Wendt

Illustrations by Aptara Inc.

Typeset in FrutigerLTStd 11/13 pts. by Aptara Inc.

Printed in Dubai

A catalogue record for this title is available from the British Library.

Contents

Contents

Getting the most from this book

Welcome to the *Explore PSHE for Key Stage 4 Student Book*. The Explore PSHE series is designed to help young people grow and develop as individuals, and provides a wide ranging Personal, Social, Health and Economic education course that is mapped to the statutory 2020 Relationships, Sex and Health Education curriculum.

The course takes an active learning approach, which means that you, the student, will be invited to participate and contribute to the lessons in a variety of different ways.

In terms of how this book is structured, each chapter is made up of a series of lessons. The chapters and lessons are all numbered, but your teacher may decide to deliver the lessons in another order, catered more specifically to the individual needs and aims of your school.

The following features have been included to help you get the most from this book:

Learning outcomes

Learning outcomes highlight what you will have learnt by the end of each lesson, and help you track progress throughout the course.

Starter

Starters include a short activity to help introduce you to each topic and get you thinking.

Activity

Activities throughout the book will ask you to engage with the material in many different ways, from group activities to word sorts.

Sources, ranging from illustrations and photos to newspaper extracts and information from websites, will provide the basis for activities, and stimulate discussion within the class.

What am I going to learn in PSHE?

Let's find out!

Source 1 What is PSHE all about?

Acknowledgements

Hodder Education would like to thank the following organisations for their invaluable input and reviews:

Chapters 2 and 3 were kindly reviewed by Brook. Brook is a sexual health and wellbeing charity, and has been at the forefront of providing wellbeing and sexual health support for young people for over 50 years. Find out more at **www.brook.org.uk**.

Chapter 4 was kindly reviewed by Drugs and Me. Drugs and Me is an educational website providing freely accessible, unbiased, and non-judgemental harm reduction information for alcohol, tobacco and other recreational drugs. Find out more at **www.drugsand.me**.

Chapter 5 was kindly reviewed by Mind, a mental health charity, providing advice and support to empower anyone experiencing a mental health problem. They campaign to improve services, raise awareness and promote understanding. Find out more at **www.mind.org.uk**.

Chapter 8, lesson 8.3, was kindly reviewed by Mermaids. Mermaids supports children and young people up to 20 years old who are transgender and/or gender diverse, and their families, and professionals involved in their care. Find out more at **www.mermaidsuk.org.uk**.

By the end of this lesson you will:

- understand why 'rules' and group agreements are important in the context of PSHE lessons
- have contributed to the development of a class 'group agreement'.

Starter

Think back to Key Stage 3

Think back to your PSHE lessons in Key Stage 3, brainstorm the different topics you looked at.

1. How have these helped you?
2. What other topics do you think you need to revisit or learn about now that you are in Key Stage 4?

Personal, Social, Health and Economic education (PSHE education) is part of our personal development. Personal development happens throughout our lives – in school, when we are with our friends, working, shopping, socialising and so on.

PSHE education is part of personal development that happens in the school curriculum. The Relationships, Sex and health Education curriculum (from the government) is also covered across the twelve chapters.

These Programmes of Study are supported in twelve chapters:

1 Introducing PSHE education

2 Relationships

3 Sex, sexuality and sexual health

4 Alcohol, tobacco and other drugs

5 Emotional wellbeing and mental health

6 Healthy lifestyle

7 Risk and safety

8 Identity

9 Communities

10 Planning for the future

11 Finance

12 Business and enterprise

Each chapter is divided into a series of topics that include a range of issues for you to consider. The topics are designed to:

- help you focus on the main points you need to learn by providing you with learning outcomes and structuring the activities around them

- give you the opportunity to develop the skills you need through a variety of activities

- encourage you to feel confident in sharing your thoughts and feelings in a supportive atmosphere.

Many of the PSHE themes and topics require collaboration and teamwork. Therefore it is important to develop a group agreement establishing how you can work together effectively.

Your teacher may decide to undertake a summative assessment task in some or all of the chapters. These will be linked to the End of Key Stage Outcomes for PSHE education. This will give you feedback on how you are progressing through the course.

PSHE education deals with real-life issues that affect all of us, our families and our communities. It engages with the social and economic realities of our lives, experiences and attitudes. Could there be a more important subject to study?

Activity 1

Establishing a group agreement

1 In pairs, discuss the purpose of a 'group agreement' in your PSHE lessons and write down your ideas about what should be included, for example, respect for others' opinions.
2 Share your ideas as a class, explaining why each point is important as part of a group agreement.
3 Use the ideas from your own list and others in the class to devise 'rules' that will form your group agreement, for example, everyone is entitled to their own opinion and we should be respectful of this.
4 As a class decide on the final 'rules' for your class group agreement.

Activity 2

Cross-curricula links

How does PSHE support your learning in other subjects?

Discuss your ideas with a partner.

By the end of this lesson you will:

- be able to describe different types and levels of relationships
- be able to explain different roles within relationships
- be able to identify factors that make relationships successful or difficult
- understand the importance of rights, responsibilities and respect in relationships.

In our daily lives we observe all sorts of relationships around us. Television dramas and soap operas show different relationships, as do films, books, music videos and advertisements.

Starter

Relationships in the media

List all the different relationships you have seen in films, TV, books and advertising. For example: *The Simpsons* – family, *Modern Family* - same-sex relationships.

Friends – fun ones and annoying ones!

Parents

Someone who is a good listener

Teachers

Professionals who help us – doctors, nurses, police, teachers, etc.

People we see around in the community

Source 1 Different types of relationship

Activity 1

What about you?

1 Think about yourself – what different types of relationships do you experience in your life? Using Source 2 as a guide, create your own diagram that highlights the relationships you experience.
   a Start with yourself, and represent some of your relationships with little drawings and/or names or initials, using distance from yourself to indicate the significance of the relationship.
   b Put up to 20 people in the diagram, including both close and distant relationships, and good as well as difficult relationships.
2 Choose one person from your diagram with whom you have a significant relationship and answer the following questions:
   a What type of relationship is it? (friend, family, work and so on)
   b Why is it significant?
   c What makes it a good relationship or what makes it difficult?
3 As a class discuss:
   a Why are close relationships important?
   b Are close relationships important to everyone?

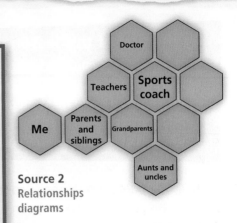

Source 2
Relationships diagrams

Relationships are the 'building blocks' for our lives as we experience them every day, and the success of these relationships can have lasting impacts on our present and future, although more often than not we take them for granted. Sometimes we are fortunate and a good relationship just happens – you 'click' with someone. Most relationships, though, need working at and maintaining to help you and the other person relate well to each other.

Both people in a relationship need to think of their interaction as a combination of **rights and responsibilities**. These two concepts go together. At some level every relationship involves both rights and responsibilities.

Think about this everyday example:

As a student I go to school to learn. I have the right to expect that the teachers plan and deliver their lessons appropriately, mark my work and provide me with feedback so I know how to improve. So they can do this effectively I have a responsibility to behave in an appropriate manner, complete work on time and act on the improvement feedback I am given.

Activity 2

Relationships need work

1 How important are 'rights and responsibilities' in a relationship? Can you give a similar example to the teachers and student on the left?
2 A lot of young people say one of the most important elements of a relationship is 'respect'. What does that mean to you?

Activity 3

Building good relationships

People often overlook the fact that when they are at work or school, they need good relationships. The people at work or school don't have to be your best friends, so why do you need to build good relationships with them?

By the end of this lesson you will:

- develop and evaluate strategies that can help to begin new relationships
- develop and evaluate strategies to help maintain healthy relationships
- develop and evaluate strategies to help end relationships.

In 1624, the poet John Donne used the phrase, 'No man is an island' in his prose 'Devotions upon emergent occasions'. The phrase expresses the idea that human beings do badly when isolated from others and need to be part of a community to establish effective relationships in order to thrive. Without doubt the phrase is as true today as it ever was, but beginning, maintaining and ending relationships when needed, is not always straightforward.

As a class you will have no doubt come up with a number of different skills and qualities that are needed for good relationships, and those that could cause problems. Many of these skills and qualities are initially developed during a period of a person's life known as 'the formative years'. This is often considered to be between the first 3–5 years of a person's life. During this time, basic skills, values and boundaries are instilled, which are then developed as we progress through life. Just how well these are instilled impacts on how well they develop in later life and in turn can impact on future relationships.

Starter

Relationships

Discuss the following questions with a partner and then as a class.

1　What makes for a good relationship?
2　What might make a relationship difficult?

Activity 1

Developing my own relationship skills and qualities

1　The list in Source 2 gives some suggestions of skills and qualities that we could all try and develop to help us in relationships. For each skill and quality, give yourself a score out of 5 (1 being poor and 5 being outstanding) based on how adept you think you are with that particular skill or quality. If you are not sure what the skill or quality means, discuss with a partner or teacher.
2　Now discuss your scores with a partner. Do they agree with your own reflection?
3　Choose two of the different skills and qualities and think of how and when you could try and develop these, for example, if you have younger siblings do you quickly lose patience with them? Could you be more empathetic?
4　Are some of the skills and qualities more difficult to develop than others, if so why?
5　Give examples of opportunities where a person could develop new relationships, for example, starting a new school.
6　How do these skills/qualities support someone in forming a new relationship?

Source 1 People should not be isolated – we need community

Most psychological research suggests that developing good relationships can be difficult, but once established the relationship becomes easier. However, there will be times in your life where the relationships that develop become unhealthy and not what you expect. This could be an intimate relationship with a partner, or a relationship between friends, peers or colleagues. In these instances it is important to develop strategies to end the relationship appropriately.

Skill / Quality	Score 1 to 5
Have a strong and positive relationship with yourself	
Accept and celebrate the fact that we are all different and have different views	
Actively listen to hear what other people have to say	
Give people time and 'be present' when you are with them	
Develop and work on your communication skills	
Learn to give and take constructive feedback	
Be more trusting	
Learn to be more understanding and empathetic	
Treat people as you would like to be treated yourself	
Accept appropriate change rather than being resistant to it	

Source 2

How to break up

Below are a number of strategies that researchers and psychologists have found people use to end relationships.

- **Avoidance or withdrawal**: avoiding the person, not engaging with them, not doing anything for the person, keeping conversations short.
- **Positive tone and self-blame**: preventing the person from having hard feelings, avoiding hurting the person's feelings, blaming yourself.
- **Open and honest**: openly telling the person that you wish to break up or no longer be friends.
- **Escalation**: becoming purposefully unpleasant, being demanding, dropping hints that the relationship is over.
- **De-escalation**: waiting until conditions were right for breaking up, for example, in a public space, gradually ending things, asking for a temporary break, leading to a full break up.

Source 3

Activity 2

Ending relationships

In pairs, discuss relationships you have had in the past and whether they have led to arguments and break ups – don't just consider romantic relationships. How did you end the relationship and could you have 'handled' the situation better?

Activity 3

Discussion

1. With a partner, discuss the advantages and disadvantages of each strategy in Source 2.
2. Which do you think is the best and worst strategy and why?
3. How do you think each person would feel when these strategies are used?
4. Can you think of any examples when you have seen these strategies being used? (Could be on TV or in real life.)
5. With a partner, come up with a step-by-step strategy that you think would help someone break up effectively with a partner or friend. Consider the strategies you have just read about, but also any other ideas you have. Share your ideas with the class.

By the end of this lesson you will:

- be able to explain the challenges of bringing up a family
- understand the importance of family budgeting
- explain how different people interpret the word 'family'
- understand the skills needed to be a good parent.

Ogden Nash, author and poet, 1902–1971

> A family is a unit composed not only of children but of men, women, an occasional animal, and the common cold.

> When our relatives are at home, we have to think of all their good points or it would be impossible to endure them.

George Bernard Shaw, playwright, 1856–1950

Jane Howard, children's books author

> Call it a clan, call it a network, call it a tribe, call it a family. Whatever you call it, whoever you are, you need one.

> Every family has a secret – that it is not like any other family.

Alan Bennett, playwright, screenwriter and author

Usually we would recognise a family as a group of people who are related to each other. However, people who take part in communal activities such as those shown in Source 1 often describe their social group as 'their family'.

Source 1 A sense of family

Starter

What can I say about family?

Each of the writers above has different feelings about 'family' – some funny, some cynical, some realistic. Write a couple of lines to express what you feel about 'family'.

Activity 1

What is family?

1 What do people mean when they call a social group they belong to their family?
2 How do the photos in Source 1 show characteristics of a family?

People may feel that family life gives them stability; knowing they can depend and rely on the people around them. Many people in romantic relationships choose to have children.

The Oxford English Dictionary defines this type of group as a **nuclear family**:

> A couple and their dependent children, regarded as a basic social unit.

There are also plenty of families who would not fit this definition, but carry the same legal rights as a nuclear family. For example, there are:

- extended families (including grandparents, aunts, uncles, cousins) who live together
- single-parent families
- families that comprise of people who live together and are not related in any way.

Whatever the family type, there are some general key skills that many people say are important for being a good parent. Source 2 gives a list of these.

Parenting skills

ASPIRING
Wanting their children to become the best they can be.

CONTROL AND DISCIPLINE
The ability to run the family fairly.

LOVE AND AFFECTION
Letting their children know they are loved.

MANAGING THE HOME
Budgeting, cleaning, clothing, feeding and so on.

PRAISE
Encouragement in all aspects of their children's lives.

RIGHT AND WRONG
Teaching their children a moral code to help them in life.

SAFETY
The skills to keep children safe from harm and risk.

TEMPER
Not to 'lose it' by being harsh or cruel.

TIME AND INTEREST
Spending time with their children: reading, playing, hanging out, etc.

Source 2

Activity 2

Types of family

Different family groups have different ways of behaving together:

- authoritarian – there are clear, fixed rules about what is and what is not allowed
- inconsistent – sometimes there are strict rules but at other times none
- negotiating – there is dialogue between adults (parents) and teenagers, with the young people gradually gaining more autonomy
- 'helicoptering' – parents who are overly involved in the life of their child. They tend to hover over their every movement and decision.

Which of these styles of family relationship/parenting do you think is likely to be the most successful and why? Discuss your ideas with a partner and be prepared to share with the rest of your class.

Activity 3

Parenting skills

The list of parenting skills in Source 2 is in alphabetical order. Which would be your priorities? Use a diamond nine format as shown below to place the nine skills, using position 1 for the most important. Remember that position 9 doesn't mean that skill has *no* importance.

```
        1
      2   3
    4   5   6
      7   8
        9
```

Being a good parent

What is good parenting?

1 Read Source 3. In light of what you have learned about key parenting skills, do you think these are examples of good parenting? Give reasons why or why not for each.
2 Now write a list of statements like those in Source 3 that describe a good child (teenager).

a Always buying the latest gadgets/trainers/fashions for their children.
b Being very strict about what time their children have to be back at home.
c Checking out their children's friends to see if they are a good or bad influence.
d Giving their children an allowance to spend each week – no strings attached.
e Not allowing their child to drink alcohol until they are 18.
f Expecting to know where their children are going to be when they go out.
g Allowing their children lots of freedom to make mistakes.
h Permitting their children to use illegal drugs at home, because it's safer than elsewhere.
i Controlling every aspect of their child's life and dictating their relationships and careers.
j Regularly check/monitor social media and internet use.

Source 3 Is this good parenting ... or not?

Can the good parenting skills you have been looking at be taught? Source 4 shows an extract from an organisation's website that tries to do just that. **Positiveparenting.com** offers advice on how to parent through books, podcasts, parenting-made-easy workshops and coaching.

Parenting – the most natural thing in the world?

By Debbie Godfrey – Mother, Grandma, Certified Parent Educator

I am a certified Parent Educator, bringing over 25 years of expertise in the parenting education field to the classes and workshops I provide. I teach the Redirecting Children's Behaviour parenting class.

Parents LOVE my workshops because they are practical and provide tools they can go home and use immediately with their kids. I am known for bringing compassion and humour into my teachings.

For 6 weeks you, along with up to 24 parents from all over the world, take the course together. You begin by reading the first chapter of the book. You then begin listening to the first week's lessons. You can listen to the recordings on your computer, or download them on to your phone or other devices. You will also be assigned homework based on the material. This homework is something to do with your children every week.

This course is for you if you want to:

* focus on the problem without judging the child
* resolve conflicts without power struggles
* create "genuine encounters" with children, away from the television
* teach children to solve their own problems, offering them guidance when needed
* replacing nagging, yelling, threats, bribes and guilt with effective, positive messages
* manage personal stress to increase parenting effectiveness
* assist children in becoming self-sufficient, socially responsible and self-confident.

Source 4

Born not made?

1 Why do you think organisations such as Positive Parents (see Source 4) might appeal to some parents?
2 There are different points of view about whether there should be some sort of parenting qualification. In order to drive a car you need a licence – should something similar be introduced before you can become a parent? Discuss reasons for and against it being introduced.

Managing the budget

As well as the parenting skills we have already looked at, part of good parenting is trying to manage the home well, including budgeting. One of the issues that can often cause conflict and arguments in a family is money: Who's bringing it in? Who's spending it? Is there enough to go around? Budgeting well and planning family finances may help avoid these sorts of conflict.

MONEY COMING IN	£			
Parent('s') take-home pay	3,400			
Working children's contributions	125			
Other sources (savings, investments, etc.)	100			
Family allowance	135			
			TOTAL INCOME £	3,760

MONEY GOING OUT	£		
BASICS	£	LUXURIES	£
Mortgage/rent	1,000	Lunches/coffees (not home-made)	150
Council Tax	145	Eating out/social drinking	200
Gas	40	Outside entertainment, e.g. cinema	50
Electricity	80	Sport and recreation such as the gym or swimming	70
Water	38	Hair/beauty	100
Phone (bundle)	25	Home entertainment	30
TV Licence	15	Satellite/cable subscription	50
Groceries	600	Magazines/newspapers	15
Clothing	150	Mobile phones	40
Babysitting	80	Lottery tickets/betting	10
Vehicle running costs	220	Vet's bills	25
Other travel costs	50	Gardening	15
Insurance (house/life/car, etc.)	80	Cleaner	80
Other, e.g. pocket money	25	Holidays	200

TOTAL BASICS EXPENDITURE £	2,548	TOTAL LUXURIES EXPENDITURE £	1,035

NON-MORTGAGE DEBTS	£		
Credit/store card repayments	65		
Loan repayments	140		
Other			
TOTAL NON-MORTGAGE DEBTS £	205		
		Total expenditure £	3,788
		TOTAL INCOME minus TOTAL EXPENDITURE (£3,760 – £3,788)	-£28.00 (DEBIT)

Source 5 Monthly financial planner

Activity 6

Family budgeting skills

Look at Source 5, which shows a family budget planner. The areas listed are those that the family regularly spend on; and right now they're having difficulties managing. Offer some suggestions for where and how the family – including the children – could make savings.

Activity 7

Impacting on others

1 Most people could change one thing about their own behaviour to make life at home easier and happier with others. Assuming you're not perfect, what one thing would you change about yourself?

2 Imagine you had to write a postcard of appreciation to your parent/carer. What one thing would you most value them for? Do you let them know this?

By the end of this lesson you will:

- understand issues that can make relationships unhealthy or damaging
- understand laws that support people in unhealthy relationship situations
- be able to explain why respect is an important part of a relationship
- be able to identify potentially abusive relationships.

Abuse

Abuse can take many different forms and levels of severity. In pairs make a list of the different types of abuse that can occur, for example, sexual abuse.

Over the past few years, there has been a significant increase in the number of incidents of different types of abuse reported to the police and other organisations such as the NSPCC. You will probably be able to recall stories you have heard on the news which relate to these different types of abuse.

10,000 living at risk of domestic violence

1,343 new child abuse cases in 3 months

THE FULL HORROR OF GANG VIOLENCE EXPOSED

Domestic violence will now include 'mental torture'

ABUSE OF ELDERLY IN CARE HOMES

Source 1 Headlines

Childline define sexual abuse and harassment as:

Sexual abuse is when someone is forced, pressurised or tricked into taking part in any kind of sexual activity with another person. It can include lots of things like rape and sexual assault, sexual harassment, online grooming and domestic abuse or violence.

Examples of sexual abuse include:

- being touched in a way you do not like without giving permission or consent
- someone flashing or exposing themselves to you online or offline

- being forced to have sex (intercourse)
- look at sexual pictures or videos
- do something sexual or watch someone do something sexual
- it can also include sexual exploitation (being pressured into having sex with someone in return for getting something like money or drugs)
- sexting or child pornography.

Sexual harassment is a type of bullying in a sexual way. It can leave you feeling humiliated, embarrassed, self-conscious and frightened.

Sexual harassment is when you are made to feel uncomfortable if somebody:

- pinches or grabs your breasts and private parts
- spreads sexual rumours about you
- says inappropriate or sexual things about the way you look that make you feel uncomfortable
- calls you names such as slut, tart, whore or man whore
- objectifies you by talking about your body parts
- takes your clothes off when you don't want them to
- touches you in a way you don't like
- forces you to kiss somebody or do something else sexually.

Source 2 From Childline's guidance about sexual abuse. Childline provides counselling for young people up to their 19th birthday

Grooming

One of the areas of reporting that has increased most dramatically is 'grooming' and sexual abuse of children. A government report into child sexual abuse (December 2018) highlighted a 700 per cent increase in referrals of online child abuse cases since 2013. In August 2016, police had reported an average of 3500 referrals a month. Childline have seen a 20 per cent increase in the number of children accessing their help about sexting. 12,200 counselling sessions were given to children to tackle the issue of online abuse. There is also concern that there is under-reporting of these issues, and that this is just a small fraction of what is actually going on.

Case study

Grooming – a mother's story

I was a social worker specialising in working with vulnerable children when it happened in 2012 and I thought I was pretty clued up when it came to child protection. I didn't want my daughter to have Facebook: the legal age is 13 and she was still only 11. Her older sister had it and all the kids at school were talking about it; she said she felt left out. She would pester me daily: 'It's not fair, Maddy has it, Kate has it, why can't I have it? Please mum please mum please mum.' I knew in my gut that I shouldn't have let her, but eventually and regrettably I gave in – I was sick of the relentless arguments. I noted her password and told her that I might occasionally check her account. I warned her about paedophiles. The groomer's method was simple yet highly effective. He managed to make 'friends' with other girls at her school and by the time he came to request my daughter, they had 32 mutual friends.

So what does a paedophile look like? The picture she saw on his profile was a blurred photo of a teenager wearing what looked like school uniform. He called himself Jack Smith. My daughter wasn't sure if she knew him, but they had 32 mutual friends, so she presumed that she did, and she accepted him.

We only found out who he was at the trial. He lived just around the corner from us. I have no idea if he specifically targeted my daughter because he knew who she was or whether it was just a terrible coincidence. I'll never know. He was sentenced to five years in custody.

He was the smiling assistant who helped us in our local supermarket. Late 20s, tall, thin and geeky looking, not your average looking paedophile, whatever that is. He'd have a joke with us and offer to help with our packing. I can remember commenting to a friend: 'Have you seen that new guy in the shop, he's so nice and friendly.' So charmed was I by him. This was the man who groomed my daughter.

It began with him sending her friendly messages, a few jokes, some emojis thrown in – all relatively innocent. This progressed to asking her to turn the webcam on; I didn't even know Facebook had a webcam option at that time. She resisted at first, but they were building up a friendship and in the end she felt obliged. She told me that she was also intrigued. She turned the webcam on but didn't show herself, instead she placed one of her teddies in front of the screen. The fact that she had a teddy bear on hand to be able to do this breaks my heart repeatedly.

From *The Independent*, 6 February 2017

Domestic abuse

Another area of relationship concern is the increase in reported incidents of domestic abuse/violence. According to figures released by the Office for National Statistics (ONS), in March 2018, an estimated 2 million adults aged 16 to 59 years experienced domestic abuse throughout the year (1.3 million women, 695 000 men). The police recorded 599 549 domestic abuse-related crimes during the same period, which was an increase of 23 per cent from the previous year. This suggests that the police are improving their identification and recording of domestic abuse incidents and that there is an increased willingness by victims to come forward.

Source 4 Incidents of reported domestic abuse are increasing

The number of people being prosecuted has increased as has the conviction rate which in March 2018 was at 76 per cent. However, as with grooming, there is still an ongoing concern that the issue is being under-reported and this is still a fraction of what is actually happening.

Expect respect!

Awareness of abuse in relationships has often been focused on adults – but a recent NSPCC survey showed that 1 in 5 teenagers have been physically abused by their boyfriend or girlfriend.

Abuse in teenage relationships may involve:
- physical violence
- pressuring a partner into having sex
- controlling behaviour
- unnecessary jealousy or anger.

Source 3

Case study

Domestic abuse – Jennifer's story

I married my ex-husband after only four months of being together. We had both been married before so when he suggested that we shouldn't involve our families and get married quickly, I could see his point. He had two children from his previous marriage as did I, so during our first summer together we all went on holiday together. Whilst in the restaurant he saw me talking to one of the waiters. At the bar later that evening he was very quiet and 'moody' with me. When we returned to the room he hit me, accusing me of flirting with the waiter. The next morning I packed my bags to find another hotel. He chased after me, apologising repeatedly to the point I actually felt sorry for him, and really thought he was sorry.

We moved house a few months later, at which point things got progressively worse. He would push and shove me, although never when the children were around. The pushes and shoves became slaps and punches. At one point he smashed my head into a chest of drawers, and hit me with a hole-punch from our study.

Whilst you may not think things can get worse, this is when he began 'gaslighting' – making me question my own sanity by doing various psychological things to me, for instance convincing me that I was putting my work before my family. So I reduced my hours at work, but this meant that he had even more control over me, because if things weren't perfect at home he would abuse me even more – once he hit me because a fork was in the knife compartment of the cutlery drawer.

Another example was when we wanted to get together with my parents and sister. I would arrange something that he agreed to and when I reminded him, he would deny all knowledge or state that I hadn't explained myself clearly, but that it was done now and he would come along so as not to disappoint. He made me constantly feel that it was my fault, and over time I lost my self-esteem and confidence. I would try and keep the peace and let him have his own way as I didn't want to be hit.

At work I developed a reputation as being clumsy due to the bruises that would appear. He appeared a perfect gentlemen to others, but eventually I confided in a colleague, hoping they would know what to do.

I did have some dark thoughts including suicide, but my children kept me going, and eventually as I fell in the hall after he had tripped me, something changed. I kept repeating 'I'm not going to take this anymore, I'm not going to take this anymore'. He laid into me again at which point one of my daughters and one of his heard the thumping and came downstairs grabbing his arm. He knocked them both over, before sitting down in the living room to watch TV as if nothing had happened. Until the knock came on the front door, I hadn't realised my other daughter had called the police; he was arrested, convicted of assault and is not allowed near me.

It didn't occur to me that I was suffering domestic abuse – in my head, that was something that happens to someone else, not to me. But domestic abuse can happen to anyone.

Activity 3

Discussion

1 Having read the case study about Jennifer, discuss the following points with a partner, before sharing your discussions as a class.
   - What is domestic abuse/violence?
   - What did Jennifer's ex-partner do to her? Think about physically and mentally.
   - Why didn't Jennifer feel able to leave with her children?
   - What were the short- and long-term impacts for Jennifer and her children of their experience?
   - Why do you think that some victims of domestic abuse/violence don't report it?
   - What consequence do you think Jennifer's ex-partner should receive for his actions?

By the end of this lesson you will:
- be able to describe signs of exploitation in relationships
- be able to recognise signs of harm and risk in relationships
- know how and where to seek support for relationships.

Starter

Who's out there?

Apart from the regular emergency services (police, ambulance and fire brigade), what other support agencies do you know of?

In the previous topic you explored some of the ills of modern society, including problems associated with grooming and domestic violence. By learning more about the agencies available to help, we can understand more. Perhaps in the future we may even find we are a 'signpost' to these agencies for friends, neighbours or acquaintances that are experiencing problems.

Sharon and Paul

Sharon and Paul are 16 and have been seeing each other for a few months. They've been getting along really well until Paul started putting on the pressure. In front of their friends and family, Paul is really charming – but when he and Sharon are alone, it's a different story: He wants to have sex even when Sharon doesn't. He says things like 'If you don't do what I want I'm going to tell everyone that you're frigid' or 'How will you feel when I tell the whole school that you're a lez?' As well as sexual harassment and bullying, his behaviour is now beginning to show that he could be physically violent, for example, he forcibly kissed her and fondled her breast.

Support for Sharon
www.thesurvivorstrust.org

Source 1

Ebu and Grace

Grace has really enjoyed going out with Ebu – that is until last weekend when his behaviour suddenly changed. They were out together and Grace remembered that she'd promised to text her best friend. She started to do this and Ebu grabbed her wrist and said: 'What do you think you're doing? I didn't say you could do that.' It turns out he thinks he can and should control who Grace speaks to. His tone was so menacing that Grace was frightened of responding.

Support for Grace
www.actonitnow.co.uk

Source 2

Simon

Simon is constantly abused by his partner: the abuse varies from aggressive comments and emotional bullying to hitting, kicking and slapping. Simon's partner also takes pleasure in belittling him in front of their friends and acquaintances. Simon feels embarrassed because although he's heard about 'domestic violence' he thought it only happened to women. This means he feels he can't talk about it.

Support for Simon

www.mensadviceline.org.uk

Source 3

Jamila

Jamila, 22, has learned that her parents are planning to make her travel to Pakistan. They want her to marry a man they had betrothed her to several years ago. This was done without her knowledge; she's never met the man she's meant to be matched with. She had been put into the engagement against her wishes. Her parents had gone quiet about this and she'd hoped they had listened to her opinions but quite recently the subject has been raised again. It is still not what she wants.

Support for Jamila

www.fco.gov.uk/en/travel-and-living-abroad/when-things-gowrong/forced-marriage

Source 4

Irina

When Irina was seven, her mum married again.

At first she got on well with her new stepfather but then he began to shout all the time and scare her. He occasionally slapped her mum and before long he was hitting Irina too. She had a lot of problems with school while this was going on and was often covered in bruises from her stepfather. She was embarrassed about what was happening at home and felt she couldn't talk to anyone about it.

Later on Irina found a boyfriend, but after a while he became very controlling about what she wore, who she spoke to and who she was friends with. Because she had seen this happening to her mum, she thought it was normal, but when she asked her friends if this had happened to them, they said it hadn't.

THE HIDEOUT
www.thehideout.org.uk
until children are safe

Support for Irina

www.thehideout.org.uk

Source 5

Activity 1

Who can they speak to?

Read Sources 1–5. Each of the five people needs help and support. Choose one and research the helping agency listed for them. Plan a presentation about the agency. The presentation should include the following:

- name of the agency
- who it's run by and for
- how it can be accessed
- example(s) of how they've helped others.

Make your presentation as practical and helpful as possible. Include (if there are any) drawbacks or restrictions to using the agency in question. Your overall aim is that other students will be able to take away:

- an awareness of exploitation in relationships
- an ability to recognise harm in risky situations and know where to turn for help and support.

How can our school help?

With the increase in incidents of domestic abuse and grooming, schools are playing an essential role in supporting young people through difficult experiences. As a student you should be able to approach any member of your school staff with a concern and they in turn can make a 'safeguarding' referral. Safeguarding is a term used in the UK to define the laws and measures in place to allow people to live free from abuse, harm and neglect, particularly children, young people and vulnerable adults.

Staff in your school will receive regular training about safeguarding, including the signs that someone could be the victim of abuse or be experiencing other difficulties, and how to make a referral to the school safeguarding team should they have a concern. The initial concern could be raised by a member of staff, as they may have noticed a change in behaviour, mood or appearance of a student; directly by the student to a member of staff; or by someone from outside the school who has witnessed or become aware of a concern. Once a safeguarding referral has been made, the relevant school procedures will be followed to establish if the concern is a safeguarding issue.

To establish this, the school will speak to the student about whom the concern was raised, and where possible, to others involved if it is appropriate to do so. However, it may not always be possible to speak to others involved as this could cause further problems for the student concerned. In an incident such as this, other organisations may be contacted by the school to help support, such as social services, police and child and adolescent mental health services (CAMHS).

Activity 2

New to me

Which agency/agencies didn't you know about until today?

Source 6 You should be able to approach a member of staff if you have a concern

Sometimes the safeguarding referrals that are made may turn out to be nothing serious; however, it is important that they are investigated thoroughly and the correct procedures followed so as not to put someone into a further position of risk, violence or other situation that could affect their physical or mental health.

Activity 3

The signs of potential safeguarding concerns

1   Make a list of possible signs that could indicate someone is experiencing difficulties, for example, a friend always seems tired in the morning and tells you that they don't have time for breakfast as they are having to get their younger siblings ready for school.
2   Look through your list and rank the examples into a priority order that you would raise as a safeguarding concern with your teacher.
3   Your friend confides in you about an issue that you think is of concern to their safety, but they ask you not to tell anyone – what would you do?

It is important to remember that no matter how trivial you think an issue might be, you should always raise your concerns if someone is potentially at risk.

To reduce risks further, anyone that works closely with children has to undergo criminal record checks, known as the Disclosure and Barring Service (DBS). They will also be trained in safeguarding. This includes sports coaches, Guide and Scout leaders and other organisations that provide children with a service – even taxi and bus drivers are being trained to spot possible safeguarding concerns.

Source 7 Anyone working with children must be DBS checked

Activity 4

Discussion

1   Stories similar to those you have read about over the last few pages, regularly make the news headlines. What impression does this give you of the society you live in?
2   How far do you agree with these two points of view?
    • 'Most people are good people'
    • 'It won't happen to me'.

By the end of the lesson you will:

- be able to state the age of consent and explain what consent means
- be able to describe the laws around consent
- be able to identify when consent is and is not given in a range of scenarios.

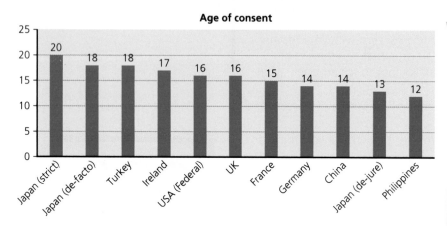

Source 1 Graph showing age of consent around the world

When beginning sexual relationships, it's important to be aware of the laws surrounding sex and sexual consent.

The age of consent for sex in England is 16. This applies to all young people regardless of their sexual orientation.

A child under 13 is not legally capable of consenting to sexual activity and therefore any offence under the Sexual Offences Act 2003 involving a child under 13 is very serious and should be taken to indicate a risk of significant harm to the child.

Consent is about giving permission for something to happen or an agreement to do something. Nobody has the right to make a person go further than they want to. Everyone has the right to say no, at any point, whoever they are with. If someone wants to have sex but their partner doesn't, they must absolutely respect their feelings.

A person under the age of 18 cannot consent to sex if it is with a person who has a duty of care or is in a position of authority or trust, such as a teacher, doctor or lecturer.

Starter

Age of consent

The age of consent for sex in the UK is currently 16. Do you think it should be changed? If so, why?

'No' means no!

If someone says 'No', it means no! Having sex with somebody who is unable to give their consent is against the law.

This might include:

- someone who has a disability such as their mental capacity is lower than their biological age, or for whatever reason, is unable to express their wishes
- someone who is 'out of it' for any reason (for example, through alcohol or drugs). They cannot consent to having sex – so that would be breaking the law too, this includes any kind of sexual activity such as kissing or fondling
- someone is asleep or unconscious they are unable to give consent.
- if they are threatened or forced, they do not have the freedom to consent.

Activity 1

Consent scenarios

Read through each of the scenarios below in Source 2. For each, consider the questions that follow.

Based on an activity by the Government of Western Australia Department of Health.

Paul and Jane

Paul and Jane are both 16 and have been together for three months. Jane has implied to Paul that she will dump him if he does not have sex with her in the next few days. She is fed up with waiting. Paul really likes her and is afraid of losing her and so agrees to have sex.

1 Is consent given?

2 How would Paul feel?

3 Do Jane's actions show mutual respect?

4 How could the situation be managed?

Isabelle and David

Isabelle, 17, and David, 16, meet at a mutual friend's party. They get on well and clearly have things in common. David reaches over and kisses Isabelle, who enjoys it. David then starts to touch Isabelle who is OK with it at first, but starts feeling unsure and asks David to stop. David ignores her and continues.

1 Is consent given?

2 Can a person withdraw consent?

3 Can consent be given for some things but not others?

4 What will they both take from the experience?

Jamal and Laila

Laila goes to the movies with Jamal. Laila is 15 years old and Jamal is 17. After the film Jamal and Laila make out. Jamal then asks Laila if she wants to have sex with him. Laila replies 'yes' as she feels ready. Neither have been drinking.

1 Is this consent?

2 Is there a problem with a 15 year old and 17 year old having sex?

3 Would the outcome be different if Jamal was 15 and Laila was 17?

James and Ivan

James and Ivan have been together for a year. They know each other really well as they are also next door neighbours. James is 16 and Ivan is 17. Recently they have been talking about having sex. They discuss what is OK with each other and what isn't OK.

1 Is consent given?

2 Is this legal?

3 What will they take away from the experience?

Source 2 Sexual activity scenarios

Getting educated

Young people aged 16 have reached the age of consent. However, at 16 many students have reported that they have not received much in the way of sex education and have characterised the education they have received in the past as too little, too late and too biological. Some young people say that it would have been good preparation for the future to have been given good, relevant, non-judgemental sex and relationships education.

A global study by Bristol University in 2016 found a consistency in young people's views on sex education received at school, regardless of whether they were British, American, Japanese or from elsewhere.

The study found that:

- Schools throughout the world were 'out of touch' with the experiences of their students and that students switch off because they find it irrelevant.

- Many students thought that lessons about sex and relationships were moralistic, negative and overly-scientific. Students needed more support to help them deal with their emotions and feelings.

- Young women could be at risk of harassment after sex education lessons; young men were scared of revealing their lack of sexual knowledge and experience.

- Young men were often disruptive, leaving young women unlikely to ask questions and fully participate.

- There was too much focus on heterosexual relationships.

- The teaching was often poor quality because of a lack of training.

Learning about sex and relationships is preparation for the future – it doesn't mean you have to have either sex or relationships right now. Each person needs to make a personal decision about when they feel ready. Sex can be a pleasurable experience and there's nothing wrong with waiting until you're older to enjoy it.

Source 3 Talking about relationships and sex

Activity 2

Right person, right time, right place, right reason

Read statements A-J in Source 3. Choose the three statements you most agree with and explain why you agree with them.

By the end of this lesson you will:

- understand the importance of, and responsibility that comes with, sexual relationships
- be able to list a range of ways that people can show love and affection in relationships
- be able to describe some of the benefits of sexual relationships.

Sex can mean different things to different people. Whether a person is heterosexual, gay, lesbian, bisexual, questioning or unsure, it is important for them to consider carefully their own views on what sex is. Sex can refer to anything that feels sexual, not just intercourse, and this may change as a person gets older, as may their sexual interests. The most important thing to remember though is that each person must feel comfortable with any type of sexual activity they take part in and they can always say no. (See lesson 3.1 about consent.)

Teenage relationships often involve physical intimacy and sexual feelings. Romantic relationships are a major development milestone in a person's life and are linked to other developments they have had and may be experiencing such as puberty, body consciousness and independence.

Starter

Sex – why all the fuss?

Based on media reports, soap operas, music videos, and so on, what do you think is the average age that young people in the UK have sexual intercourse for the first time? Why do you think this?

Source 1 Many teenagers begin romantic relationships

As with other aspects of life, romantic relationships will have their ups and downs, and the feelings that develop are likely to feel extremely intense, due to the hormonal changes in the brain. The 'spark' or 'chemistry' as a romantic relationship blossoms can be difficult to manage, and it can be hard to distinguish between the intense, new feelings of physical attraction and the closeness that goes with being in love.

Work in progress

While a teenager's body may be developing quickly, the brain could be described as a 'work in progress', meaning that decision-making and self-regulation functions may not be able to keep up with the appearance of a mature body and for many people increasing sexual urges. These could lead to intense feelings of sexual attraction and even falling in love.

Some people do not experience sexual attraction and have no desire to have sex, while others consider sex to be an essential part of a loving and devoted relationship. For the latter it is about intimacy, pleasure and expression of love. Sexual activity may also have intellectual, physical, emotional and social benefits. A study by the University of Pennsylvania found that those that had sex more frequently had higher levels of an antibody called immunoglobulin and slept better, both of which improve a person's immune system.

Emotional health can also be affected in a positive way and sexual satisfaction has been linked with an overall better quality of life. When a person orgasms (both men and women have orgasms which are intense feelings of sexual pleasure, sometimes referred to as 'coming' or 'climaxing') it can reduce stress due to the endorphins (a type of hormone) that are released. Endorphins activate the pleasure centres in the brain creating feelings of intimacy and relaxation, which can keep depression at bay.

Sexual relationships should not be forced and only occur when both people involved are ready. There are also other ways people can show their love affection for someone.

Love	Lust
■ grows slowly	■ at first sight
■ security	■ jealousy
■ level-headed	■ distracted
■ patient	■ impatient
■ friendship	■ image
■ has a future	■ is about today
■ gives	■ takes

Activity 1

Showing love and affection

1 How do people in romantic relationships show their love or affection for each other?
2 Why do people have sex?

Activity 2

Love or lust?

As a teenager, do you think it is possible to fall in love, or is it more likely to be lust?

By the end of this lesson you will:

- understand what it means to be sexually healthy
- be able to describe different types of contraception and how they work
- be able to identify which contraceptives are most appropriate for different scenarios
- understand the signs, symptoms and causes of sexually transmitted infections (STI's)
- know how and where to seek sexual health advice.

What is sexual health?

A sexually healthy person is someone who understands that sex can have various outcomes, ranging from pleasure to transmission of sexually transmitted infections (STIs).

The sexually healthy person engages in:

- active learning
- decision-making
- communication
- behaviours

that eliminate or reduce the risk of unplanned pregnancy and/or STI transmission.

Starter

How does a person keep sexually healthy?

Read the statement of values above and answer the following questions.
To keep themselves safe, what:
1 does a young person need to know about sex?
2 does a young person need to know about relationships?
3 skills does a young person need?
4 sources of help does a young person need to know about?

> Sexual health is a state of physical, mental and social well-being in relation to sexuality. It requires a positive and respectful approach to sexuality and sexual relationships, as well as the possibility of having pleasurable and safe sexual experiences, free of coercion, discrimination and violence.

Source: www.who.int/topics/sexual_health/en/

Keeping sexually healthy

Knowing and understanding different contraceptive methods is a basic part of being a sexually healthy person. Source 1 lists a range of reliable methods of contraception.

CONTRACEPTION

Condoms

Condoms are number one for protection against STIs and 98 per cent effective in preventing pregnancy if used correctly every time sexual intercourse happens.

A condom is made of very thin latex (rubber) or polyurethane. Condoms fit over the erect penis and female condoms fit inside the vagina. Both work in the same way by catching sperm when the penis ejaculates. Some condoms are lubricated to make them easier to use.

Additional water-based lubricants can be used with condoms. Oil-based lubricants, for example, Vaseline, should be avoided as they may damage the condom.

The 'pill'

This is a widely used method of contraceptive which is swallowed. The pill prevents eggs releasing from the ovary and is 99 per cent effective at preventing pregnancy. It is reliable if it is taken regularly by the person for whom it was prescribed. If they experience vomiting or diarrhoea or is prescribed antibiotics, the 'pill' may become ineffective and a doctor should be consulted and another method of contraception used.

Contraceptive injection

This is an injection of hormones given by a nurse or doctor for those with female bodies. It is usually renewed every 8–12 weeks and the clinic reminds you when your next injection is due. The injection is 99 per cent effective at preventing pregnancy if used correctly.

IUS

The Intra Uterine System (IUS) (or coil) is a small 'T' shaped plastic device containing a hormone. The IUS is placed into the uterus by a nurse or doctor. This is a simple procedure. Once in place it is immediately effective as a method of contraception. It can remain in place for up to five years.

A similar method to the IUS is the intrauterine device (IUD). It is fitted in the same way, but unlike the IUS, it is made from copper and doesn't release any hormones.

Implant

This is a tiny stick containing a hormone. It is easily placed just under the skin in the arm by a nurse or doctor. Once in place it does not need to be renewed for three years and is 99 per cent effective at preventing pregnancy.

Emergency contraception

This should not be used as a routine method of contraception but can provide a back-up if the usual method of contraception has gone wrong. There are two types of emergency contraception. There is a pill which can be taken usually three to five days after intercourse (although more effective the sooner it is taken). These are widely available from a doctor, family planning/sexual health clinics, pharmacies and some A&E departments. Another method of preventing pregnancy is the insertion of a coil up to five days after intercourse.

Dental dams

A dental dam is a soft plastic latex square about 15 cm in size. It is used to cover the vulva or anus during oral sex. The dam prevents the transmission of sexually transmitted infections by acting as a barrier. They are available in different flavours and can be used with lubricants. They should only be used once. A makeshift dental dam can be formed by cutting a slit down the length of a condom and laying it flat.

Source 1 Methods of contraception

Scenario 1

Milly and James, who are 18, have been going out for several months. They use condoms to protect against STIs and pregnancy, however the other evening when they had sex, the condom broke.

Scenario 2

Taylor, who is 17, has been going out with her boyfriend, who is also 17, for 6 months. She confides in you that she is considering having sex with her boyfriend, but they don't know what method of contraceptive control to use.

Scenario 3

Josh, 19, tells you that he had sex with his girlfriend Emily, 18, last night, for the first time. They decided to use the withdrawal method (this means he withdrew his penis before ejaculating).

Scenario 4

Yvonne and Nina, who are both 17, have been going out for a few months and are at the point that they feel ready for sex. Neither of them is comfortable talking about contraception.

Scenario 5

Michael and William, both 18, have been together for a month and have decided the time is right to have sex. William has suggested they use a condom, but Michael is reluctant to do so.

Getting tested

It is increasingly common for people to get tested before they have sex, so they are sure that there is no risk of infection. However, this isn't always the case and sometimes things don't go according to plan and problems occur. Two of the unintended consequences of unsafe sex are sexually transmitted infections (STIs) and unplanned pregnancy. Having unprotected sex means that your sexual health is at risk. In a UK study, 15–24 year olds accounted for 61 per cent of those diagnosed with chlamydia, 36 per cent with gonorrhoea, 25 per cent with genital warts and 39 per cent with genital herpes in 2018.

Activity 1

Which contraceptive?

In groups, choose one of the scenarios outlined here. Your group should work together to develop a conversation/role play providing appropriate suggestions about which contraceptives shown in Source 1 would be most appropriate. Include conversations between any combination of the following for each scenario:

Scenario 1
• James • Milly • A friend
• A parent • A doctor or nurse.

Scenario 2
• Taylor • A friend, doctor, nurse or parent

Scenario 3
• Josh • Emily • A parent
• A friend, doctor or nurse

Scenario 4
• Yvonne • Nina • A friend
• A doctor or nurse • A parent

Scenario 5
• Michael • William • A friend
• A doctor or nurse

Activity 2

Discussion

STIs are a medical problem with an estimated 357 million new cases worldwide each year. Why do you think people are reluctant to talk about them or 'get tested'? How could this situation be improved?

STIs – Did you know …

- 70 per cent of women and 50 per cent of men who have an STI may not have any symptoms.

- Chlamydia is now the most common (yet easily curable) STI in the UK and in the last decade the number of people infected with Chlamydia has increased by 206 per cent.

- As many as one in ten sexually active young people under 25 may have Chlamydia but don't know it. There aren't always symptoms but an infection could leave you unable to have children.

- There are an estimated 20 000 HIV-positive people in the UK who don't know they've got HIV. It weakens the immune system so that the body finds it harder to fight off other infections. There is no cure, however medication can successfully control the progression and in the UK people with HIV now have the same life expectancy as those without it.

- A person doesn't need to have lots of sexual partners to get an STI – anyone who has sex without a condom is at risk.

- A study by Southampton University found that of 520 people surveyed at the local STI (genito-urinary medicine, or GUM) clinic 76 per cent stated they had had unprotected sex because they had been drinking.

If you have unprotected sex … think about the following:

- Get yourself checked out – whether you have symptoms or not. Unprotected sex leaves you open to infections.

- If you have itches, sores or blisters around your genitals, you may have an STI. No need to panic, but you do need to contact your local sexual health (genito-urinary medicine, or GUM) clinic – don't wait to see if it clears up.

- Sexual health check-ups and contraception – including condoms – are free and available to everyone in the UK.

- You can arrange a visit to a sexual health (genito-urinary medicine, or GUM) clinic any time. It is completely confidential.

- Use a barrier method of contraception (male/female condom, dental dam) every time you have sex in the future - this is the best way of making sure you don't get an STI.

- Condoms come in a wide range of sizes, flavours, colours and shapes and are available for all genders. There are allergy-free versions and even vegan varieties!

Source: Public Health England, Sexually Transmitted Infections in England, 2018

Activity 3

Signs, symptoms and solutions

In pairs, use the internet to research and produce an information leaflet about one of the following STIs: chlamydia, gonorrhoea, trichomoniasis, genital warts, genital herpes, pubic lice, syphilis, HIV and AIDS.

Your leaflet should include the following:
- information about the infection – bacteria/virus
- causes – how it is passed on
- signs and symptoms of infection
- longer term complications
- how tests are carried out
- treatment for the infection
- where and how to seek advice.

Share your findings with others in the class to gain a wider understanding of other types of STIs.

A 2013 study by The London School of Hygiene and Tropical Medicine looked at anal sex among young people. It suggested that some young heterosexual couples are having anal sex that is not enjoyable for both parties and that sometimes young women are coerced (strongly pressured) into having unsafe and painful anal sex.

The reasons for this were varied. While the young people interviewed mentioned wanting to copy what they saw in pornography, there were various other reasons such as young men competing with one another to have anal sex. Worryingly, there seemed to be a lack of concern about the levels of pain the young women might experience or whether they have their consent.

Other responses about anal sex included that there was no need to use a condom, as there is no chance of pregnancy – but of course this does not prevent sexually transmitted infections.

While raising children isn't always easy, most parents would agree that having children is an amazing thing. When you are young, you may assume that you will have children at some point in your life, and take for granted your ability to do so. However, an increasing number of people wanting families are seeking medical support to conceive as they are unable to do so naturally.

Starter

Having children

In pairs, discuss why people have children.

Peak reproductive years for women are between their late teens and late twenties. The average age of women having their first child in the UK is 28 years. By the age of 30, their ability to become pregnant starts to decline, so it is important to plan for when you want to have children, particularly if you plan to have more than one.

The UK used to have one of the highest rates of teenage pregnancies among more developed countries. As a result of improved sex education, easier access to contraception and a shift in aspirations towards education, teenage pregnancies have fallen at an astonishing rate. The Office for National Statistics (ONS) states that in 2007 there were 41.6 pregnancies per 1000 girls under 18, whereas in 2016 this had fallen to 18.9.

Activity 1

Teenage pregnancy and geography

Look at Source 1. In pairs, discuss possible reasons to explain why some areas have higher rates of teenage pregnancies.

2017

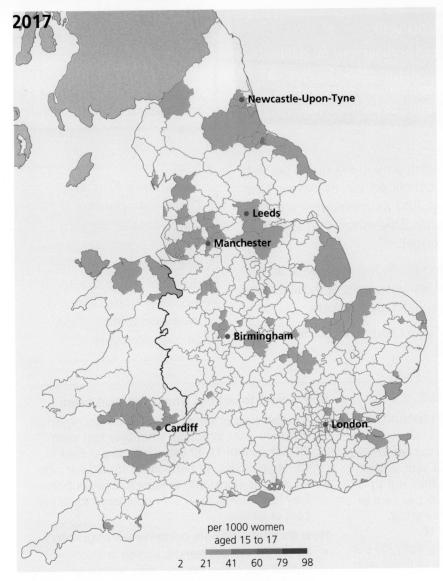

per 1000 women
aged 15 to 17

2   21   41   60   79   98

Source 1 Under 18 conception rates by local authority, 2017

Results from the National Survey of Sexual Attitudes and Lifestyles (Natsal), has shown that 1 in 6 pregnancies in the UK were unplanned and these were most likely to occur in women aged 20–34 years. While pregnancies in the 16–19 age group account for only 7.5 per cent of all pregnancies, they do account for 21 per cent of all unplanned pregnancies. This could be considered a concern for the young person as it could delay their future plans and impact on their social opportunities.

The research found a number of factors that increased the likelihood of unplanned pregnancies were:

- having sex before the age of 16
- lower educational level
- not living with a partner
- higher levels of smoking, depression and having used drugs.

Activity 2

Unplanned pregnancy

Vikki and Joe are looking forward to October – one of them has a place at Art College and the other at University. They don't live far apart and their families know each other well. Vikki and Joe have been together since Year 11 and six months ago their relationship became a sexual one. They thought they had their contraception sorted out. So, when Vikki missed a period she didn't panic. But when she missed the next one they were both shocked to find that she was pregnant.

In common with many other young couples in this situation, they faced the following options:

- abortion
- adoption
- grandparents bring up baby
- care for the baby themselves.

Consider each option and decide:
1 What might they feel about this?
2 What do they need to think about?
3 What should they do?

Activity 3

Support for me

Who would you turn to if you had a problem relating to sex or pregnancy? Why would you choose this person?

By the end of this lesson you will:

- be able to describe the impact of pornography on children and young people
- understand the impact of pornography on relationships
- be able to explain the laws relating to pornography.

Too easy?

Do you think that pornography is too easily accessible?

The online pornography industry is worth around £11 billion per year globally, reaching more people and younger people, every year. One pornographic website revealed that in 2017 its videos were watched 92 billion times in one year by 64 million daily visitors – equivalent to 12.5 videos for every person on the planet.

The internet has made access to pornography incredibly easy, and despite some measures to check and verify the ages of those looking at it, it is still extremely easy for those underage to access.

A study commissioned by the NSPCC and Children's Commissioner for England in 2017 found the following:

> The Oxford English Dictionary defines pornography as:
>
> Printed or visual material containing the explicit description or display of sexual organs or activity, intended to stimulate sexual excitement.

Who has seen online pornography?

Just under half of children surveyed reported seeing online pornography:

- At 11, the majority of children had not seen online pornography (28 per cent of 11–12 year olds).
- By 15, children were more likely than not to have seen online pornography (65 per cent of 15–16 year olds). Almost all of this group (94 per cent) had seen it by age 14.
- Boys actively searched for pornography (59 per cent) more than girls (25 per cent) of those who answered the question.

What do young people say that they feel?

- On first viewing pornography, young people reported a mixture of emotions, including curiosity, shock and confusion: curious (41 per cent), shock (27 per cent) and confused (24 per cent).
- Shock and confusion subsided on repeated viewing, whether or not pornography was deliberately sought out.
- Just over half of boys (53 per cent) who had seen pornography thought it was 'realistic' compared to 39 per cent of girls.

Some want to act out what they have seen:

- A higher proportion of the older cohort reported that they want to act out what they had seen (21 per cent of 11–12 year olds; 39 per cent of 13–14 year olds; 42 per cent of 15–16 year olds).
- Boys were more likely to want to copy activity they had seen (44 per cent compared to 29 per cent of girls).

How do young people perceive pornography?

- 50 per cent of the sample agreed or strongly agreed that online pornography 'led me to believe that sexual activities should be enjoyable for everyone involved' (54 per cent of boys answering the question and 45 per cent of girls).
- 44 per cent agreed or strongly agreed that online pornography 'led me to believe that sexual activities should be safe for everyone involved' (54 per cent of boys answering the question and 30 per cent of girls).
- 49 per cent agreed or strongly agreed that online pornography 'led me to believe that sexual activities should be agreed by everyone involved' (55 per cent of boys answering the question and 35 per cent of girls). Most young people thought pornography was a poor model for consent or safe sex and wanted better sex education covering the impact of pornography.

Source 1 The Impact of Online Pornography on Children and Young People

Activity 1

Should we be concerned?

Read the statistics in Source 1 and answer the questions below.

1 What surprises you the most? Why?
2 What doesn't surprise you? Why?
3 What (if anything) concerns or worries you about these results? Why?
4 What do you think can be done about our concerns?

Pornography and real life

The majority of the pornography that is seen online is not real. Everything from the way that people look to how and where they have sex are 'manufactured'. Thanks to plastic surgery, editing, acting and Photoshop, the women and men look very different in real life to how they look on screen.

EX-PORN STAR TELLS THE TRUTH ABOUT THE PORN INDUSTRY

Adult film performers, who have to engage in prolonged sexual acts with several partners, are at particular risk of contracting HIV and other sexually transmitted infections. In addition, many 'porn stars' report heavy use of drugs, including ecstasy, cocaine, marijuana, xanax, valium, vicodin and alcohol, leading to addiction. This, coupled with degradation and abuse (both physical and mental), means that many performers in the porn industry experience severe mental health issues.

Adapted from an article by www.covenanteyes.com

Source 2

Mental health also a concerning topic for people working in the sex industry, as Source 3 discusses.

Mental health issues have always been a big problem in the porn world, but a spate of deaths of such young porn performers raises serious questions for how women are treated in the industry.

Steve McKeown, a psychoanalyst, founder of MindFixers and owner of The McKeown Clinic, told UNILAD:

Nearly 90 per cent of women in the sex industry said they wanted to escape, but had no other means for survival and also experienced post traumatic stress disorder at rates of nearly 70 per cent, equivalent to veterans of combat war.

Most of the adult actresses should not be called 'porn stars', but instead 'porn performers', due to the fact that most of them never make it to the level of being a 'star' and are simply forced to perform, before 'ending up in poverty' and 'lucky to leave the industry with the clothes on their backs'.

These women are experiencing this constant emotional and physical trauma of sexual assault but are 'forever silenced by virtue of some decision you made at 18 to go into the sex industry, not understanding the ramifications'.

Source: Adapted from an article by www.unilad.co.uk.

Source 3

What impacts does it have?

The viewing of pornography is also having an impact on the reality of those watching, as Source 4 shows.

> A report looking at teenagers' pornography use in the UK revealed that many young men refuse to wear condoms during sex, because it doesn't happen in the online videos they watch. There was also an increase in the number of people practising anal sex. More concerning is another report which stated that 40 per cent of college students in India regularly watched 'rape porn' with over 75 per cent admitting that it 'instils a desire to rape women'.
>
> Young women were also affected by watching porn as they compared themselves to the women in the video, reflecting on their own body appearance and sexual performance and acts against what they saw online.
>
> Source: Adapted from an article by Paula Beaton www.expertrain.com.

Source 4

There is clear evidence that online pornography for some can have an impact on sexual desires, expectations and instils extreme urges, which can then be difficult to satisfy, leading to addiction. In the USA, a study by the American Psychological Association in 2018 found that eighteen per cent of men surveyed said that they were addicted or unsure if they were addicted to pornography – nearly 1 in 5 equating to 21 million of US men. In March 2019, UK, Addiction Treatment Centres, which run clinics across the UK, said it had seen the numbers of teenage pornography addiction admissions more than triple in three years.

Source 5 Relationships can break down

So, what are the impacts of the increased viewing of pornography?

> The following have been identified as impacts of regularly viewing pornography:
> - affects intimacy in relationships
> - reduce sexual connection with a partner
> - contributes to increased relationship breakdowns (pornography is cited in 50 per cent of divorces)
> - less likely to be sexually satisfied
> - think about sex more frequently
> - affects self-esteem when comparing own body to actors in videos
> - children becoming more sexually active at a younger age
> - promotes 'bad attitudes' particularly towards women – 'sex objects'
> - less progressive attitudes towards gender roles
> - increases craving for more pornography as dopamine is released in the brain – teenagers are particularly susceptible
> - may find it difficult to form relationships in the future
> - more likely to engage in risky sexual behaviour, for example, not using a condom which may contribute to a rise in STIs.

Source 6 The impacts of viewing pornography

Activity 2

Agree or disagree?

Read through Sources 2, 3, 4 and 6.
1   Your teacher will give you a handout which contains a number of statements. Having read the sources, cut out the statements and arrange them on a continuum of 1–10 depending on how strongly you agree with them. 1 being strongly disagree and 10 being strongly agree.
2   Compare your results with a partner. What were the similarities and differences? Discuss your findings.

Are the laws strict enough?

Concerns over the ease of access to pornography, particularly for those under 18, has led to the UK government intervening. In 2018 it was announced as part of the Digital Economy Act, that:

■ a new age check will be built into websites and other online platforms that provide pornography on a commercial basis to the people of the UK

■ businesses that fail to comply will be fined up to £250,000

■ to access pornography, you will be required to enter credit card details upon loading the homepage of a website, which will confirm proof of age, but you will not be charged.

However, it was announced in October 2019 that the government had decided to scrap their plans as they could be easily 'bypassed' and only applied to websites that charged for their services.

Activity 3

Are the laws strict enough?

1   Do you think the original government plans for an age check would have been successful?
2   What could be done to restrict access by under 18s to pornography?

By the end of this lesson you will:

- understand the law about different types of drugs
- be able to explain the drug supply chain and its impacts
- know the signs, impacts and where to seek support with regards to 'county lines' and 'cuckooing'
- be able to describe and evaluate the risks associated with drug taking.

From ancient times to the present day, people have used drugs for all sorts of purposes. Drugs have always been around – particularly to help cure illnesses and avoid pain, and also for pleasure.

Mushroom stones crafted in Guatemala in 1000 BCE are believed by many to represent psychoactive mushrooms (though these are not original Mayan stones).

Starter

Why do people use drugs?

Make a list of all the reasons why you think people take drugs. Consider legal and illegal drugs.

When the word 'drugs' is mentioned, it is often assumed people are talking about illegal drugs. However, the medicines we use to make ourselves better are types of drugs, as are alcohol and tobacco, all of which are legal. When taking any drug, it is important to be aware of potential side effects and the impact they can have on your health, both good and bad.

Have we created a 'pill-for-every-ill' culture?

In our society we do seem to be using legal drugs quite regularly. Illegal drugs are also prevalent and can cause emotional and physical health problems, and sometimes have a negative impact on society. Whether legal or illegal, there is no drug that is risk free.

Activity 1

A drug-using society?

It has been said that we live in a drug-using society. Leaving out illegal drugs, discuss whether you think this is true. Use the following ideas to help your discussion:

- complementary therapies (for example, plants such as echinacea and arnica) draw on natural remedies to prevent or treat illnesses
- alcohol and tobacco are widely used recreationally by large numbers of people – people can become dependent on them
- using over-the-counter medicines (bought from pharmacies, supermarkets and so on) is a standard way of dealing with feeling unwell
- walk-in centres and GP practices can supply prescription medicines to treat a wide range of problems – some people become over-reliant and may develop dependency.

Activity 2

Drugs risks – true or false?

Decide if the following statements are true or false.

a Possessing magic mushrooms is not against the law.

b LSD is not addictive.

c One of the main dangers of cannabis is the state of intoxication it produces.

d Injecting can be one of the most dangerous ways of taking drugs.

e Solvent sniffing is not illegal.

f It is illegal for a 16-year-old to smoke cigarettes or e-cigarettes.

g If a teacher knows a pupil has used illegal drugs they have to tell the police.

h The police can enter a school and make a search without a warrant.

i If a pupil tells a teacher that they have used illegal drugs the teacher is legally bound to tell their parents.

j If a person buys one ecstasy tablet for a friend with the friend's money – that person could be charged with supplying drugs.

1. **Hitesh** is growing cannabis plants in his greenhouse. He probably won't bother to harvest them.		2. **Nancy's** parents are really 'laid back' about cannabis. They used to smoke it themselves but don't anymore. They don't mind Nancy smoking cannabis in their house – on her own and/or along with her friends.	
3. **Jermaine** is into athletics in a big way and takes steroids to improve his performance. He also gets steroids for **Chantal** but doesn't make any profit out of selling them to her.		4. **Lee** bought what he thought was ecstasy from a dealer at a club. In fact it is ketamine.	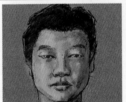
5. **Tony** and **Lorraine** are 17. They go into their local pub and order a pint of beer and a pint of lager at the bar. A police officer walks in.		6. **Damian** is 14 and regularly buys poppers (nitrite) from a local shop.	
7. **Jennifer and her friends** buy NPS (psychoactive substances – formerly known as legal highs) from another student at their college.		8. **Jacob** and **Noah** buy spice (a synthetic/human-made cannabis) from a local dealer. They sometimes smoke it at the park.	

Source 1 What's the risk?

Activity 3

What's the risk?

Look at Source 1 and answer the following questions:

1 Is anyone committing an illegal offence?

2 Are there any other risks being taken? What are they?

The drug economy

When it comes to information and discussion about drugs, many people focus on laws controlling their sale and penalties for using them. However, the whole picture is far more complex. Sometimes we talk about a 'drug economy'. The next activity explores the bigger picture of drugs; their supply, sale and use.

AFGHAN HILL FARMER

You farm in a remote hill area of Afghanistan. You have to work hard to make a living to keep your young family. If you grow sugar beet or a similar crop, you will get a government subsidy – but even taking this into account your annual earnings would be £500 per year. If you grow opium poppies you can sell the raw opium for £200 per kilo. Farming this way you can earn £1500 per year. The only world you know is the Afghan mountains. You are not aware of what happens to the crop once it leaves your hands.

INDIVIDUAL USING HEROIN

You were introduced to heroin by a friend. You liked the effect. Now you have become dependent on it and need it regularly to keep going. You spend a lot of time working to get the money to buy supplies. You have your troubles in life and heroin seems to take away the worries. You would actually like not to be dependent on it but stopping is hard. You think you are harming nobody but yourself. You make sure that you always use clean injecting equipment that you don't share with anyone else.

DRUG PRODUCER

You buy the crop from the hill farmers and process it to make pure heroin. You are proud of the quality of the heroin you produce; it is pure when it leaves you and not mixed with any other substances. Some producers do make more money by mixing in cheaper substances but you realise this could be dangerous for the individual using the drug. You work hard and if caught could spend a lifetime in jail. What you buy from the farmer for £200 you sell to an international gang for £5000. You live a good life.

DRUG SUPPLIER (DEALER)

You run a group of street suppliers who buy the heroin from you and sell it on to people. You believe people should be free to choose how they spend their money and if some want to use it to buy heroin you will supply it. You can make £80,000 profit on a kilo of heroin when it is sold, broken down into small 'bags'. You believe you help poor poppy farmers make a living.

DRUG SMUGGLER

You can make £5000 per shipment for bringing a kilo of heroin through customs. The risk is very high if you are caught, but you like the excitement of finding new ways of smuggling. You believe you are providing a service and think people should be free to use or take what they like.

Source 2 **A drugs supply chain**

Activity 4

The drugs supply chain – values, responsibilities and harm

In groups of four, look at the characters in the drugs supply chain and consider the questions below:

- What is their role in the drugs supply chain?
- What do you think they value?
- How responsible are they for the continuance of the drugs supply chain on a scale of 1 to 10 with 10 being the most responsible?
- Who is causing the most harm? (harm could be considered in relation to health, society, relationships, etc.)

- What would be the best solution to disrupt the drugs supply chain?
- What would be the implications of this on each character?

Makes notes and be prepared to feedback your ideas to the rest of the class.

County lines and cuckooing

Considerable awareness has been raised over increasing trends in drug dealing known as 'county lines' and 'cuckooing', which are having significant impacts across the country.

Drug dealers may move into new areas to sell their products. The link from their old home to their new home is known as the 'county drug line'.

The dealers look for vulnerable housing tenants and take advantage by taking over their home and using it as a base for their criminal activity. This is known as 'cuckooing'.

The gangs involved are often violent and intimidate people into doing what they want. They also target children and recruit them to move drugs and money for them. In some cases children as young as 10 are exploited and forced to carry drugs between locations, usually on trains or coaches to a buyer.

Source 3

Activity 5

County lines and cuckooing

Source 3 provides some information about county lines and cuckooing. What else do you think you need to know about these issues? Make a list of questions you would want to know the answers to. For example, in which parts of the country does it happen?

Use these websites to research answers to your questions:
www.childrenssociety.org.uk/what-is-county-lines
www.fearless.org/en/campaigns/county-lines
www.police.uk/

Activity 6

Offering advice

You have been given the chance to offer the government some advice about ways to reduce the negative effects of drugs. Choose one piece of advice and justify why you have chosen it.

By the end of this lesson you will:

- understand and evaluate the risks associated with alcohol consumption
- be able to explain the laws relating to alcohol consumption
- be able to explain why young people have differing views about the use of alcohol
- know how and where to seek support for alcohol use.

Suggested limits have been put in place to enable people to make healthy choices about how much alcohol they consume:

In March 2017 the Chief Medical Officer for England, recommended to adults who drink regularly or frequently (that is, most weeks), that:

- To keep health risks from alcohol to a low level it is safest not to drink more than 14 units a week on a regular basis.

- If you regularly drink as much as 14 units per week, it is best to spread your drinking evenly over 3 or more days. If you have one or two heavy drinking episodes a week (known as 'binge' drinking), you increase your risks of death from long-term illness and from accidents and injuries.

- If 15 to 17 year olds drink alcohol, it should be rarely, and never more than once a week. They should always be supervised by a parent or carer.

- If 15 to 17 year olds drink alcohol, they should never exceed the recommended adult weekly limit (14 units of alcohol). 1 unit of alcohol is about half a pint of normal-strength beer or a single measure (25ml) of spirits. A small glass of wine equals 1.5 units of alcohol. Read more about alcohol units.

Source 1 How many units?

Starter

Over the limit?

1   Using the illustration in Source 1, what could the following groups drink in a week and still stay within the recommended maximum number of units?
    a   adults
    b   teenagers

To help understand the number of units in alcohol, producers of alcoholic drinks have been encouraged to display the number of units in their drinks clearly on the label. There are also apps available so consumers can track their alcohol consumption, such as Drink Aware

Activity 1

Party, party!

1   Look at Source 2. Which of the responses do you
    a   most agree with?
    b   least agree with?
2   Give reasons to explain your answers.
3   Write a response that reflects your views.

and Drinks Meter, that enable you to track units and calories of drinks, and set targets to reduce your intake.

The law relating to underage drinking is intended to prevent people under 18 buying alcohol. However, underage drinking is common, and the parent in Source 2 is struggling to decide what to do about her daughter's request.

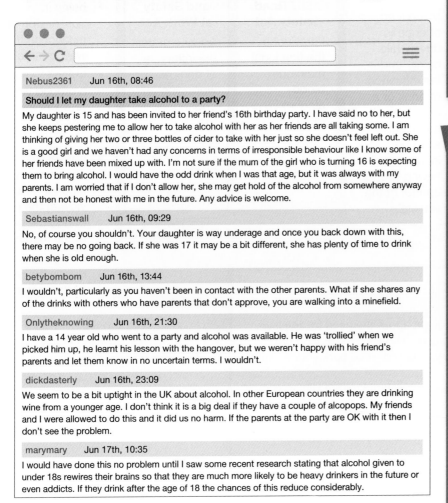

Nebus2361   Jun 16th, 08:46

Should I let my daughter take alcohol to a party?

My daughter is 15 and has been invited to her friend's 16th birthday party. I have said no to her, but she keeps pestering me to allow her to take alcohol with her as her friends are all taking some. I am thinking of giving her two or three bottles of cider to take with her just so she doesn't feel left out. She is a good girl and we haven't had any concerns in terms of irresponsible behaviour like I know some of her friends have been mixed up with. I'm not sure if the mum of the girl who is turning 16 is expecting them to bring alcohol. I would have the odd drink when I was that age, but it was always with my parents. I am worried that if I don't allow her, she may get hold of the alcohol from somewhere anyway and then not be honest with me in the future. Any advice is welcome.

Sebastianswall   Jun 16th, 09:29

No, of course you shouldn't. Your daughter is way underage and once you back down with this, there may be no going back. If she was 17 it may be a bit different, she has plenty of time to drink when she is old enough.

betybombom   Jun 16th, 13:44

I wouldn't, particularly as you haven't been in contact with the other parents. What if she shares any of the drinks with others who have parents that don't approve, you are walking into a minefield.

Onlytheknowing   Jun 16th, 21:30

I have a 14 year old who went to a party and alcohol was available. He was 'trollied' when we picked him up, he learnt his lesson with the hangover, but we weren't happy with his friend's parents and let them know in no uncertain terms. I wouldn't.

dickdasterly   Jun 16th, 23:09

We seem to be a bit uptight in the UK about alcohol. In other European countries they are drinking wine from a younger age. I don't think it is a big deal if they have a couple of alcopops. My friends and I were allowed to do this and it did us no harm. If the parents at the party are OK with it then I don't see the problem.

marymary   Jun 17th, 10:35

I would have done this no problem until I saw some recent research stating that alcohol given to under 18s rewires their brains so that they are much more likely to be heavy drinkers in the future or even addicts. If they drink after the age of 18 the chances of this reduce considerably.

Source 2

Activity 2

More than health risks

1   Most people think of the risks associated with misusing alcohol as health risks, for example, liver disease and mental health problems. However, it poses risks for other things as well. Give examples of negative effects alcohol has for each of the following:
    a   family
    b   the law
    c   employment
    d   finance
    e   social relationships.

Activity 3

Drink problems

Most areas have local organisations that people can turn to if they need help and support with alcohol-related problems.

1   Find out what local support groups exist in your area, what they do and how they can be accessed. The NHS has a directory that lists local alcohol addiction support groups (**www.nhs.uk/servicedirectories**).

2   Use the information you find to produce a poster for your school's PSHE notice board about local alcohol support groups and the service they provide.

Alcohol and the law

Because alcohol causes health problems as well as wider problems for society, the government has created laws about its use in order to try and minimise the harm it can cause. Legislation about alcohol has been developed over many years to address:

- the prevention of crime and disorder
- public safety
- the prevention of public nuisance
- the protection of children from harm.

Source 3 shows the timeline of some laws related to alcohol.

> a) Set a minimum price for alcohol to reduce sales to young people.

> b) Supermarkets to stop multi-buy/bargain deals of cheap alcohol.

Source 4 Ideas for new legislation around alcohol

1872 Licensing Act

Made it an offence to be drunk while in charge of carriages, horses, cattle and steam engines.

1898 Inebriates Act

Prevention of sale of alcohol to habitual drunkards.

1930 Road Traffic Act

Made it an offence to drive while being 'under the influence of drink or a drug to such an extent as to be incapable of having proper control of the vehicle'.

1967 Road Safety Act

Introduced the first legal maximum blood-alcohol (drink-driving) limit in the UK and the breathalyser.

1974 Health and Safety at Work Act

Anyone under the influence of drink at work who endangers the health and safety of themselves or others is liable to prosecution.

Football Matches

Acts in 1980 and 1985 created offences including:

- being in possession of alcohol on the way to matches
- trying to enter a ground when drunk or in possession of alcohol
- possessing or consuming alcohol within view of the pitch during the period of the match
- being drunk during the period of the match.

Source 3 Legislation about alcohol

Activity 4

More laws?

1 What problems do you think brought about the need for the laws in the timeline in Source 3? In groups, choose one law and discuss reasons why you think this law was passed. Feed back your reasons to the class.

2 Alcohol consumption and problems associated with it still appear to be increasing. Do we need more legislation? The ideas in speech bubbles in Source 4 at the top of these pages are all possible areas for new legislation about alcohol. Give an example of an argument for and against each.

3 Are there any other realistic and more workable solutions (other than more legislation) to reduce the problems associated with alcohol consumption?

c) Reduce hours that pubs and clubs can open and sell alcohol.

d) Total ban on consuming alcohol on the street/in public places/on public transport.

e) Restrict happy hours or irresponsible price-based promotions; for example, women 'drink for free' promotions are still all too common.

g) Display alcohol in designated and separate areas; for example, no more displays by the checkout.

f) Restrict the way alcohol is sold, such as offering drinks in small as well as large glasses or measures; for example, too often only one size is offered or a large is automatically given.

1988 Cyclists: The Road Traffic Act

Made it an offence to cycle/ride a bike under the influence of drink or drugs.

1991 Road Traffic Act

Made it an offence punishable by a compulsory prison sentence to cause death by careless driving when under the influence of drink or drugs.

1997 Confiscation of Alcohol (Young Persons) Act

Gave police the power to confiscate alcohol from under-18s drinking in public places (streets, parks, etc.) and creating disorder.

2001 Criminal Justice and Police Act

- On-the-spot penalties for a range of offences including public drunkenness, disorderly behaviour while drunk in a public place and consumption of alcohol in a designated alcohol-free zone.
- Local authorities have power to designate public places as alcohol-free zones.
- Allows 'test purchasing' of alcohol – under-18s being used by police to test the willingness of licensees to sell illegally to the underage.

2003 Licensing Act

An offence is being committed if:

- under-18s buy or try to buy alcohol
- over-18s buy alcohol on behalf of under-18s (this does not apply if the child is 16 or over and is bought beer, wine or cider by someone aged 18 or over, but only to drink with a meal in the dining or restaurant area of a pub when accompanied by someone aged 18 or over)
- an under-18 is sent to buy alcohol on your behalf.

Activity 5

Minimum alcohol pricing

In 2018, Scotland introduced minimum alcohol pricing legislation. The new law set a minimum price for drinks depending on how many units of alcohol they contain. A two litre bottle of cheap cider containing 14 units would previously cost around £2.50. Under the new law, it will now cost at least £7.50.

Do you think this law should be introduced in other countries within the UK?

By the end of this lesson you will:

- know about the numbers of people consuming alcohol, tobacco, legal and illegal drugs
- be able to explain how and why people become addicted
- know how and where to seek support for addiction.

How harmful are alcohol and tobacco?

A report, *Global Statistics on Alcohol, Tobacco and Illicit Drug Use*, published in 2018 stated that 'Alcohol and tobacco are by far the biggest threat to human welfare of all addictive drugs'. The researchers looked particularly at: how common the use of these substances were; how many people were dependent on them; how many deaths are related to these substances and how much ill health is related to these substances.

The smoking of tobacco was found to have the biggest impact globally on human health, while the use of illegal drugs the least. The report was quick to point out that the results should not be misinterpreted as illegal drugs being safer: illegal drugs also have their own unique risks but are used significantly less by comparison to alcohol and tobacco. Another point they make is that while some illegal drugs can also be very harmful to individuals (e.g. heroin), alcohol and tobacco have an added societal harm (e.g. fights in the street from alcohol or second-hand smoke from tobacco) which is much less present in other drugs.

Starter

Time to reclassify alcohol and tobacco?

The report makes the case that if tobacco and alcohol had only been discovered a short time ago, they could both be added to the list of Class A illegal drugs.

Considering the fact that alcohol and tobacco have a greater impact on human health than other drugs, should they be added to the list of Class A drugs?

Report findings

In the past year ...

- Nearly twenty per cent of adults reported drinking heavily in a 30 day period.
- Around fifteen per cent of adults smoked daily in any 30 day period.
- About four per cent had used cannabis and less than one per cent used opioids, amphetamines or cocaine in the past year.
- Out of every 100,000 people in the world, 111 will die from tobacco use, 33 will die from alcohol-related causes and 7 from illegal drug use.

Source 1

The use of tobacco, alcohol, legal and illegal drugs can lead to increasing tolerance, dependence and addiction of the substance being used, as well as cross-dependence and cross-tolerance.

- **Tolerance:** Tolerance happens when the person's body becomes used to the drug, lessening the effect. This means that more of the drug required is to reach the effect they are seeking.

- **Cross-tolerance:** Cross-tolerance occurs when the tolerance to a drug produces tolerance to another drug with similar effects. For instance, there is cross-tolerance between alcohol and a group of drugs called anxiolytics.

- **Dependence:** Dependence means that when a person stops taking a drug, their body will go into 'withdrawal'. Withdrawal can be physical or mental symptoms that can be mild or even life threatening. An increasing concern is the number of people who are becoming dependent on prescription drugs as they use them over a long period of time. People that are dependent on drugs are not necessarily addicted. A habit crosses into an addiction if the person loses control of their behaviour and experiences strong uncontrollable cravings. The relationship between dependence and addiction is complex, and it can be difficult to discern between the two.

- **Cross-dependence:** Cross-dependence occurs when a drug reduces withdrawal signs and symptoms that result when another drug stops being used.

- **Habit:** A habit is a particular behaviour that a person engages in as part of a routine. These can be adaptive (e.g. things that a person might do in everyday life, such as moderate levels of exercise), or maladaptive (e.g. things that a person might do that have a negative or non-productive impact, such as excessive levels of drug taking).

- **Addiction:** Addiction is a complex psychobiosocial disorder (i.e. it is affected or influenced by the mind, body and society). It is a long-term, or chronic, relapsing disorder that is characterised by cravings, habitual drug seeking and unpleasant subjective experiences during abstinence. In the development of addiction, tolerance and dependence build up. A person that can't stop taking a drugs even though it is having negative consequences is considered to be addicted.

Why do people become addicted?

Developing an addiction means that people will crave and therefore seek out substances regardless of the cost, not just financially, but also socially as they risk hurting friends and family.

Addiction is long-lasting and even for those that have successfully quit, there is always a chance the addiction could return, which is known as a 'relapse'. Addiction isn't a choice, and is now considered a disorder affecting behaviour and the nervous system.

Activity 1

Factors increasing a person's risk of addiction

Source 2 shows that the brain clearly plays a key role in the addiction of any substance. Make a list of other factors that you think could increase a person's risk of becoming addicted.

Addiction and the brain

A well-adapted brain switches on the appropriate 'brain circuits' as we encounter different scenarios, for example, exercising or meeting with friends makes you feel good, therefore your brain will motivate you to repeat those experiences. When you are in danger, a well-adapted brain will tell your body to react quickly to avoid any potential harm. When you are tempted to buy something you know that you can't really afford, the frontal regions of your brain will help you decide if the consequences are worth it.

However, when a person is developing addiction, their 'brain circuits', behaviour and environment are affected. Regarding the brain, alcohol and other drugs change the circuitry of the brain. Brain areas involved in reward, motivation, memory and cognitive control are affected. There are changes in the neurons, which make up the brain. The function and number of what are called 'neurotransmitters' and 'receptors' can change dramatically.

The way that the different brain areas talk to each other is modified.

Additionally, the brain chemistry is unbalanced during withdrawal, which results in unpleasant experiences. People crave drugs to reduce these feelings. This may lead to a vicious cycle that strengthens habits.

Source 2

45

Legal drugs

While addiction to alcohol, tobacco and illegal drugs has received regular coverage for many years, there is growing concern about the increasing rate of addiction to legal or 'prescription' drugs.

In January 2018, Public Health England launched a review into the growing problem of prescription drug addiction, following reports from the NHS that stated 1 in 11 patients in England is being prescribed medication that could be addictive or difficult to come off.

Some prescription drug misusers begin with legitimate prescriptions given to them by their doctors, but many others are becoming addicted without legally obtaining a prescription. The drugs may be bought on the street, online or may be stolen.

In the UK, the most abused prescription drugs include:

- painkillers

- sleeping pills

- weight loss pills

- anti-depression medication

- anti-anxiety medication

- ADHD medication.

Drug misuse – symptoms

If used properly, prescribed medication can manage symptoms well. However, prescription drugs can also be misused. Signs of prescription drug misuse or addiction include ...

- frequently thinking about your medication
- taking larger doses than the doctor has prescribed
- taking medication for reasons not prescribed for
- seeking prescriptions from more than one doctor
- seeking repeat prescriptions more frequently
- multiple prescriptions or altered forms
- you may feel angry if people talk about it with you
- withdrawal symptoms become apparent e.g. restlessness, cold sweats, etc.

Source 3

When the National Health Service (NHS) was introduced in 1948, there was little concern over alcohol, tobacco and drug addiction. A report by the National Drug Treatment Monitoring System revealed that in 2017 nearly 300,000 people in England were in contact with drug and alcohol services.

Activity 2

More money needed

Using Sources 3, 4 and 5, discuss whether you agree that cuts to the funding of services providing support to people with alcohol and drug addiction is responsible for increasing numbers becoming addicted. What do you think could help prevent young people experiencing substance use and addiction?

Facts about the treatment of alcohol, tobacco and illegal drug misuse and addiction

- In the early 2000s the UK was seen as the global leader in preventative services for misuse and addiction.
- Since 2010 there has been a government shift from drug substitutes such as methadone to abstinence (going without) in treating addiction.
- There has been a large increase in the dependency on voluntary organisations offering support, rather than the NHS.
- Spending on alcohol and other drugs services has been cut by 25 per cent since 2013.
- In 2014 the cost of treating those who misuse drugs and alcohol was estimated to be £4 billion.
- Accident and Emergency visits due to alcohol poisoning doubled between 2006 and 2014.
- In 2015, one in three GP visits were linked to alcohol consumption.

Source 4

Activity 3

Write a letter

Imagine you are working for a charitable organisation that supports young people with issues regarding alcohol, tobacco and illegal drug abuse. Write a letter to your local MP, giving your proposal for an increase in funding for addiction and preventative services. Use Sources 1–5 and your own research to help with your letter.

Government accused of cutting vital drug and alcohol services as £43m slashed from addiction budgets

The Government has been accused of presiding over 'staggering cuts' to vital alcohol and other drugs services, forcing town halls to slash £43m from addiction budgets in one year.

Shadow Health Secretary Jonathan Ashworth, who has spoken out about growing up with an alcoholic father, will accuse ministers of 'failing some of the most vulnerable' in a conversation with the comedian Russell Brand at a fringe event during the Labour conference.

MPs were moved to tears in Parliament earlier this year when Mr Ashworth spoke of caring for his dad, also called Jon, from when he was just eight years old, as his father was often too drunk to buy food or walk him home from school.

'The long-term effect will be growing addiction problems in society and increases the long-term costs for the health services.'

Analysis of official figures revealed 106 of the 152 local authorities in England are cutting £28.4m from their drug treatment budgets in 2017/18 compared with the previous year, while 95 councils are slashing £6.5m from their funds for alcohol abuse over the same period.

Karen Tyrell, of the charity Addaction, told *The Independent*: 'We know that drug and alcohol services make a massive difference for people who are often at their lowest point when they come to us. It really does save lives.

'Every £1 spent on drug treatment saves £2.50, so every penny taken away needs to be carefully considered.'

Source: *The Independent*, 25 September 2017

Source 5

Activity 4

Discussion

Some people believe that as alcohol, tobacco and illegal drug abuse are 'self-inflicted', patients using the NHS to help them recover from related illnesses should pay additional tax. Do you agree?

By the end of this lesson you will:

- reflect on your own mental health and be able to explain the factors that affect it
- understand and be able to explain the importance of good mental health
- understand and be able to explain the impacts of poor mental health.

Starter

Good mental health

Make a list of characteristics that you would expect someone with good mental health to have.

Emotional wellbeing and mental health, particularly for young people, has been of growing concern in recent years, with research showing increasing numbers being diagnosed with a mental health condition and seeking support.

What impacts on our mental wellbeing?

'Emotional wellbeing, is a term used to describe a person's mental state. This can include how they are feeling and how well they can cope with day-to-day life. A person's wellbeing is 'dynamic' which means that it can change, hour to hour, day to day, week to week and so on.

The charity Mind identifies someone that has 'good' mental wellbeing as being able to:

- feel fairly self-confident and have good self-esteem
- feel and express a range of emotions
- build and maintain good relationships with others
- feel connected to the world around them
- cope with stress in everyday life
- be productive at school, college or work
- react and adapt, and deal with change or uncertainty.

Someone with poor emotional wellbeing may struggle in one or more of these areas.

But what can cause a person to have poor mental health?

A person's mental health can be affected by a number of different things and vary from person to person.

Source 1 gives some examples of everyday events that can affect a person's mental health.

Loss of loved ones

Problems at home or in relationships

Bullying

Source 1

In addition to events that cause stress in our everyday lives, research also shows that there are other things that could make a person more likely to experience a problem with their mental health. These include:

- worrying about what's happening in the world, like things you hear about in the news
- being a carer for a friend or family member
- long-term physical health conditions
- trauma, such as being a victim of crime or an accident
- being homeless or living in poor housing
- living in poverty
- discrimination
- being abused.

Activity 1

What impacts our mental wellbeing?

In pairs, look at the images in Source 1. For each image discuss with your partner how you think the examples could impact on a person's mental wellbeing.

Activity 2

Improving mental health

Read through Sources 2 and 3. In pairs, discuss the following:

1 Which fact were you most surprised about?
2 Why do you think the number of young people experiencing anxiety or depression has increased so rapidly?

3 Some research suggests that mental health problems experienced by adults often begin when they are young, or are influenced by childhood experiences. In your opinion is enough being done to promote good mental health among your age group?

What do the statistics tell us?

75% of adults with a diagnosable mental health problem experience the first symptoms by the age of 24.

Children from low-income families are four times more likely to experience mental health problems than children from higher-income families.

Among LGBTQ+ young people, 7 out of 10 girls and 6 out of 10 boys described experiencing suicidal thoughts. These children and young people were around three times as likely as others to have made a suicide attempt at some point.

In 2015, 22% of young people aged 15 reported having ever self-harmed. Young women in this age group were three times more likely to self-harm than young men.

1 in 5 young people aged 16–24 experience a common mental illness such as anxiety or depression at any one time.

In the last 20 years, young women's experiences of anxiety and depression have increased by around 38 per cent, whereas young men's experiences of the same conditions have decreased by around 2 per cent in the same period.

Every £1 spent on group cognitive behavioural therapy for anxiety in adolescence produces benefits of nearly £7.

Source 2 Research by the Centre for Mental Health

A report to MPs in Source 3 on the next page highlights concerns about access to government-funded support for young people with mental health problems. However, remember that many other support groups are available including charities such as Mind, Rethink and Heads Together who all offer free and easily accessible advice.

A report by a committee of MPs is concerned about the mental health of the UK's young people. One in eight 5- to 19-year-olds have a mental health problem and an increasing number of 5- to 15-year-olds are reported to be suffering from emotional disorders. As a result, their life chances are dramatically affected.

Even more worryingly, only a third of children/young people who have mental health problems are receiving vital treatment from the NHS. Some young people are told they are not ill enough to receive treatment and others have to wait for far too long – in some cases years.

One priority that has been identified is ensuring the right staff are in place and the committee has also recommended that NHS England provide annual updates on:

- how many young people were referred for treatment, the waiting time for treatment, and the human cost to those who did not receive treatment
- the progress being made in schools in setting up mental health support teams
- the progress in recruiting more mental health support workers for children and young people
- what is being done to prevent and treat mental health problems much sooner for children and young people.

Source 3 Concerns that MPs have with regards to children receiving the mental health support they need

Types of mental health problems

When we talk about mental health and diagnosing mental health problems, it is important to be able to tell different problems apart, so that people can be given the best treatment and support. 'Time to change' is a UK charity that works to end mental health discrimination and stigma. They encourage people to learn more about mental health so we can feel more confident in talking about it and listening to others, and if someone we know is showing signs of poor mental health we can support them in getting help.

Activity 4

Coping with poor mental health

1 Use the Youngminds website (https://youngminds.org.uk/) to find out about people who have been affected by poor mental health, such as the mental health problems listed in Source 4. Their stories are about experiences and how they cope with poor mental health.
2 As you read your story, make a note of the following and be prepared to explain to others in your class.
   a What is the name of the person?
   b What challenges were they facing?
   c What emotions do you imagine they were feeling?
   d How are they coping with the problem now – what's changed?

Activity 3

An action plan

How would you go about improving the mental health for people in your school, including students and staff? Put together an action plan/proposal as to how you would do this. Include the following:
- Why is there a need to improve mental health?
- What are the key areas you would focus on?
- Who would be involved?
- What new facilities/resources would you need?
- How would you evaluate if your plan is successful?

Activity 5

What about my own mental health?

Anyone who is worried about their own mental health should ask for help and support. We should also all try to look after our own mental health every day. The list below provides the Top 10 Tips for Good Mental Health. Copy out the list and for each tip rate how well you do this on a scale of 1–5 (1 being poor, and 5 being good).
1 Eat a balanced diet and avoid too much caffeine
2 Get plenty of sleep, with less screen time at night
3 Avoid alcohol, smoking and drugs
4 Get outside and benefit from the sunlight
5 Working out what makes you stressed and managing it
6 Be physically active
7 Make friends and talk to people
8 Make time for something you enjoy
9 Do kind things for others
10 Ask for help when you need it

Anxiety is what we feel when we are worried, tense or afraid – particularly about things that are about to happen, or which we think could happen in the future.

Occasional anxiety is a normal human experience. But if your feelings of anxiety are very strong, or last for a long time, they can be overwhelming. You might also experience physical symptoms such as sleep problems and panic attacks.

Bipolar disorder (once called manic depression) mainly affects your mood. With this diagnosis you are likely to have times when you experience: manic or hypomanic episodes (feeling high); depressive episodes (feeling low); and potentially some psychotic symptoms.

Everyone has variations in their mood, but in bipolar disorder these swings can feel very extreme and have a big impact on your life. In between, you might have stable times where you experience fewer symptoms.

Depression is a feeling of low mood that lasts for a long time and affects your everyday life. It can make you feel hopeless, despairing, guilty, worthless, unmotivated and exhausted. It can affect your self-esteem, sleep, appetite, sex drive and your physical health.

Eating disorders are not just about food. They can be about difficult things and painful feelings which you may be finding hard to face or resolve. Lots of people think that if you have an eating problem you will be over- or underweight, and that being a certain weight is always associated with a specific eating problem, but this is a myth. Anyone, regardless of age, gender or weight, can be affected by eating problems.

The most common eating disorder diagnoses are anorexia, bulimia, binge eating disorder, and other specified feeding or eating disorder (OSFED). But it's also possible to have a very difficult relationship with food and not fit the criteria for any specific diagnosis.

Obsessive-compulsive disorder (OCD) is a type of anxiety disorder. The term is often misused in daily conversation – for example, you might hear people talk about being 'a bit OCD', if they like things to be neat and tidy. But the reality of this disorder is a lot more complex and serious.

OCD has two main parts: obsessions (unwelcome thoughts, images, urges, worries or doubts that repeatedly appear in your mind); and compulsions (repetitive activities that you feel you have to do to reduce the anxiety caused by the obsession).

Personality disorders are a group of mental health problem where your attitudes, beliefs and behaviours cause you longstanding problems in your life. If you have this diagnosis it doesn't mean that you're fundamentally different from other people – but you may regularly experience difficulties with how you think about yourself and others, and find it very difficult to change these unwanted patterns.

There are several different categories and types of personality disorder, but most people who are diagnosed with a particular personality disorder don't fit any single category very clearly or consistently. Also, the term 'personality disorder' can sound very judgemental.

Phobias are an extreme form of fear or anxiety triggered by a particular situation (such as going outside) or object (such as spiders), even when it's very unlikely to be dangerous.

A fear becomes a phobia if the fear is out of proportion to the danger, it lasts for more than six months, and has a significant impact on how you live your day-to-day life.

Schizophrenia views on schizophrenia have changed over the years. Lots of people question whether it's really a distinct condition, or actually a few different conditions that overlap. But you may still be given this diagnosis if you experience symptoms such as:

- psychosis (such as hallucinations or delusions)
- disorganised thinking and speech
- feeling disconnected from your feelings
- difficulty concentrating
- wanting to avoid people
- a lack of interest in things
- not wanting to look after yourself.

Source 4 Types of mental health problems

Activity 6

What helps?

Think about things that you find helpful or unhelpful when you're struggling. Write a list, or draw your suggestions.

By the end of this lesson you will:

- know the signs and symptoms of stress
- reflect on sleeping habits
- be able to describe strategies to manage stress effectively
- develop routines for dealing with exam pressures.

Starter

How do they feel?

1 Imagine a scenario where someone is really worried about their school work. They've tried talking to their parents but they just say the person needs to work harder. They are also having problems at home because their parents are arguing a lot. They feel very upset and stressed and it is all getting too much to manage.
  a How would they feel?
  b What physical and emotional signs might you notice if someone is struggling/going through a difficult time.

Body issues   Exams

Bullying   Dating – or not

Drugs   Spots

Friendships   School work

Source 1 Lots of things to deal with!

Sometimes it feels like everything's happening at once and that's stressful (Source 1). But this stress doesn't have to pile up until it feels out of control. Taking time to acknowledge each issue and recognise what's happening can be helpful – so can being proactive and creating an action plan to use in those difficult times.

Exam pressures

Now it's time to address the big one – exams! Your teacher can give you a worksheet showing some suggestions for preparing for exams and keeping stresses at bay.

Exercise

One method of managing feelings of stress and anxiety is exercise. A report published in *The Lancet Psychiatry Journal* in 2018 said that physical activity lasting 45 minutes, three to five times a week, can reduce poor mental health. It was found that all physical activities, including child care and housework, were beneficial to mental health. People who took exercise experienced 1.5 fewer 'bad days' each month compared to people who did no exercise. Team sports, aerobics and cycling had the best positive impact on mental health.

Sleep

Another method of managing feelings of stress and anxiety is to make sure you get enough sleep in order to function well during the day. However, as Source 2 illustrates, sleep can be a problem for some young people.

Activity 1

If only there'd been more time

Most young people have different tips or techniques they use to reduce stress. What three methods to manage stress and anxiety would you pass on to a friend?

Activity 2

Pulling it all together

Look at the worksheet your teacher gives you. What do you think of the suggestions for preparing for exams and keeping stresses at bay? Score each suggestion out of 5, with 5 being 'yes, that really works' and 1 being 'not much use'.

Activity 3

Breaking a sweat

1 Think back over the past five days. For each day make a list of the physical activity that you did. Is it enough?
2 Are you missing opportunities for further physical activity? For example, walking to school rather than being dropped off.

- 'Even though there is an epidemic of tiredness in society, people don't view sleep as a priority.' (Gordon Cairns, Govan High School in Glasgow)
- 'Sleep is crucial to repair, growth and the consolidation of knowledge and memory. It's no magic revelation.' (Jane Ansell, Director of Sleep Scotland)

- Two-thirds of children are not getting enough sleep, with some getting as little as five hours a night. They say they feel sleepy, but don't make the connection with the need to go to bed earlier.
- Going into bedrooms at a decent time is not sufficient if children stay awake for hours watching television, playing computer games, texting or surfing the internet.
- 'Media invasion has a severe social and neurological impact. Flashing images from the computer, TV or mobile phone screens interfere with the body's production of melatonin, a chemical that helps trigger drowsiness.' (Mandy Gurney, Millpond Sleep Clinic, London).
- Sleep is a learned behaviour. Just as there have been improvements in healthy eating behaviours, so good sleep habits can become the norm.

Source 2 Sleep facts

Activity 4

Zzzzzzzzzzz

Most sleep experts recommend that in order to get a good night's sleep you should follow a routine of winding down before bedtime, and that bedtime should be calm without too much stimulation. Use the outline below to create a plan that might help you to get a good night's sleep and help manage some of the problems outlined in Source 2.

TIME	ACTIVITY
Arrive home from school	
Two hours before sleep time	
One hour before sleep time	
Sleep time	Make sure your bed is comfortable and that you're warm and the room is quiet

Activity 5

Top tips

What are your top tips for facing stresses and pressures in the weeks leading up to examinations?

By the end of this lesson you will:

- be able to explain how the media influences how we see ourselves
- reflect on how your own health is affected by the media
- reflect on whether males or females feel differently about body image.

Media: Various methods by which news, entertainment, education, data or promotional messages are shared. Media includes every broadcasting medium such as newspapers, magazines, TV, music video, radio, billboards, direct mail, telephone, social media and internet.

Body image: The picture each of us has in our head of how we look – our appearance, our shape, our size – and how we feel and think about our body.

Source 1

Starter

What is 'body image'?

1 a Do you agree with the definition of body image in Source 1? Why/why not?
   b Come up with an alternative and perhaps a better definition of body image.
2 Do you think young people generally have a positive or negative body image? Give two examples to explain your answer.
3 What part do you think the media plays in forming our body image?

Throughout history there have been changing fashions in clothes and in what people perceive as 'the perfect body shape'. In modern times the media has had an increasingly strong influence on our ideas of the 'perfect body' and what we 'should' look like. It regularly discusses how far different celebrities conform to this 'perfect' image, which is often not realistic or healthy to achieve.

You may have found that the results of the last activity point to a uniformity in the way most celebrities look and are presented in the media. While the results may give an overall impression of slim people being the attractive norm (see Source 2), there are lots of ways to be attractive. Discuss whether you have ever compared yourself to a celebrity, and other ways by which a person can be seen as attractive, aside from physical appearance.

Activity 1

What is 'normal'?

In pairs:
1 Choose one of the following different categories of celebrity:
   - actors
   - sports people
   - TV personalities
   - musicians/popstars.
2 Brainstorm the names of as many people as you can think of who fit into your category.
3 Choose six people from your list and consider their appearance. Think about the following:
   - weight
   - height
   - clothes/fashion
   - hair
   - jewellery.
What do they have in common? Do you think your findings have had a positive or negative effect on you?

'Snapchat Dysmorphia': Teenagers are Getting Plastic Surgery to Look Like Selfie Filters

posed by model

Teenagers are undergoing plastic surgery to look like they do in their filtered selfies – and it may be a sign they are suffering from an underlying mental health condition.

In addition to unicorn horns and dog ears, Snapchat and Instagram also offer perfecting filters that smooth skin, thin your face, and change your eye colour – photo-editing technology that has resulted in a new mental illness scientists are calling 'Snapchat dysmorphia.'

According to plastic surgeons and researchers, patients are no longer bringing in photos of celebrities, they are bringing in pictures of their selfies – edited to look like perfect versions of themselves.

Dr Vashi said: 'A little adjusting on Facetune can smoothen out skin, and make teeth look whiter and eyes and lips bigger. A quick share on Instagram and the likes and comments start rolling in.'

The emergence of Snapchat dysmorphia comes after previous studies found social media negatively impacts self-esteem and increases the risk of mental health issues.

In a 2015 report from the Office for National Statistics, more than a quarter of teenagers who use social media for more than three hours a day were found to have problems related to mental health.

Source: *The Independent*, 6 August 2018

Source 2

The Negative Effects of Beauty Bloggers

There have been over 14.9 billion views of beauty vloggers on YouTube alone.

The most likely to watch such videos are teenage females who aspire to be like those they are watching, adapting their looks through the purchase and use of the products they see being applied by the beauty vloggers.

Whether these beauty vloggers are the best influence on teenage girls, encouraging them to base their ambitions on wearing make-up, being thin, beautiful, sexy and spending copious amounts of money on jewellery and clothing, is questionable.

Whilst those that appear on the beauty vlogs may themselves be happy and lead what they consider to be successful lifestyles, there is concern that teenage girls are being overly exposed to an environment that doesn't necessarily promote a healthy lifestyle with regards to body image and an ambition incompatible with their everyday lives.

Whilst it may be exciting to have lots of clothes and look 'perfect', the vloggers have been accused of promoting a materialistic lifestyle focusing on what you have and what you look like. This has been linked with damaging the self-esteem of young girls as they feel unhappy about their appearance as they are unable to replicate what they are watching in the beauty vlogs.

Source: adapted from https://youtubeimpactsyouth.wordpress.com/2015/02/23/the-negative-effects-of-beauty-youtubers/

Source 3

Activity 2

Media influence

1 Read Source 2. Do you agree with it? Choose three different types of media from the definition in Source 1 (e.g. newspapers, radio, tv) and for each find two examples – one which supports the article and one which disagrees with it.

2 Which examples were easier to find? What does this tell you about media influence on body image?

Activity 3

Can we ever be attractive enough?

1 Read Source 3. In what ways do you think the media has had an influence on how teenagers want to look?
2 Do you think the media target all genders equally? Give reasons for your answers.
3 Read Source 4. Using this and the other sources, discuss as a class how the media could affect a person's mental health?

The deficit model and the diet industry

The diet industry in books, fitness videos and specially prepared meals is often our inspiration to get ourselves into shape.

But have individuals ever wondered about how the industry is actually contributing to the ever-growing obesity epidemic?

Diets have become like fashion nowadays. New diets seem to pop up every few months; they have even become seasonal. People often talk about this summer's hottest diet or the autumn's secret celebrity diet.

The diet industry knows that only lifestyle changes can permanently let people live healthier lifestyles. But because we are told we only need a few weeks to reach our goal we never really adopt changes that last long.

The diet industry as a whole is a money-spinning industry that has been growing as fast as our country's waist line. The fact is the industry is selling dreams and not solutions for the obesity epidemic. Research suggests 95 per cent of slimmers regain the weight – so does the diet industry rely on failure to make its profits?

Change can only really happen when you take matters into your own hands. Empower yourself to become solely responsible for your health!

Source 4

Source 5 Diet advice has become a major industry

Activity 4

Accept who you are

How can people learn to be happy with themselves without worrying whether they conform to a certain look or not?

Activity 5

Beauty is only skin deep

List things about yourself that you like which have nothing to do with your appearance.

By the end of this lesson you will:

- identify strategies that you can use when facing new challenges
- show empathy with others when problem solving
- apply problem-solving approaches to situations in your own life.

YES or NO?

Are you feeling confident about the challenges you will be facing in the next two years?

Facing new challenges

As you change from student to adult you will continually face new opportunities and obstacles that may, at first, seem impossible to overcome. However, through being both creative and logical, and looking at things in different ways, you can succeed.

Activity 1

Will these work?

Look at Sources 1 and 2 and discuss whether these approaches to facing challenges would be useful. What are the advantages and disadvantages of the different approaches?

How to deal with a risky situation: the four Cs

When facing any challenge, here are four steps that can help a person choose what is right for them. If you know someone struggling with something challenging you can also help them by using these steps:

1 **Clarify** the issue.
2 **Consider** the problem.
3 Identify the **consequences**.
4 **Choose** the most appropriate course of action.

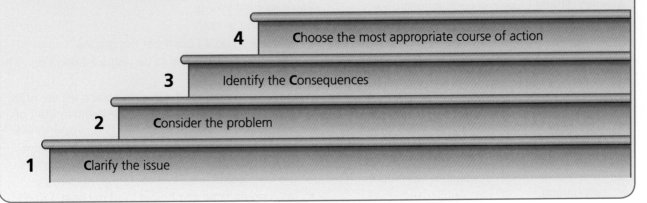

4 Choose the most appropriate course of action

3 Identify the Consequences

2 Consider the problem

1 Clarify the issue

Source 1

The emotion wheel

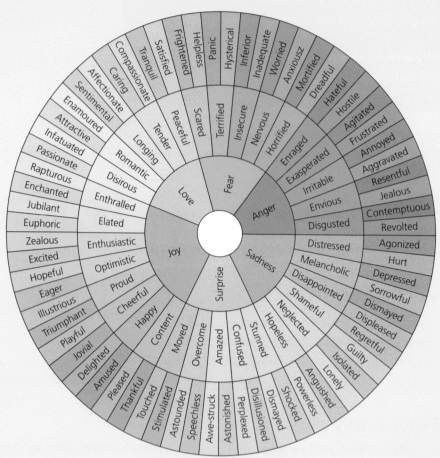

Emotion and feeling wheel

The emotion wheel was designed by psychologist Robert Plutchik. The wheel contains basic emotions, namely fear, anger, sadness, surprise, joy, love. These emotions are colour coded to express different levels of each emotion, for example, dark red represents rage, while a lighter shade of red represent annoyance. The wheel helps people to describe their emotional state which is important in developing emotional intelligence and managing mental health.

The emotion wheel encourages users to:

1 'Step back', recognise what emotion they are feeling and take some time to off-load their feelings for as long as it takes, away from the 'action'.

2 Take a deep breath or count to ten before responding.

3 With what they are feeling clearly in mind, react to the situation in a measured way – using facts and logic against their fears and concerns, e.g. thinking through the most likely outcome.

As you progress towards your exams, it is common to feel more negative or have confusing emotions. You may be thinking:

- 'I'm going to fail.'
- 'What will I do if I don't get the grades?'
- 'My parents are going to be angry if I don't do well!'

We all have moments of panic, but once we are able to recognise that and assess the problem in front of us, we can think differently:

- 'I have been revising all the topics for this exam, so will be able to answer lots of the questions at the very least.'
- 'As long as I can say I have tried my best, I can't do anymore – there are always other options.'
- 'My parents love me and will support me through whatever my results are.'

Source 2

I take care of my 15-year-old autistic brother and also my mother. My brother attends a special day school and looking after him presents challenges because he has a mental age of about six or seven. His behaviour can be fairly off the wall and unpredictable. As well as supporting my mum through her illness I take responsibility for dealing with letters, bills, phone calls and appointments because English isn't my mum's first language. My day usually starts at 5:30 am and ends at 11 pm. I don't know where to begin to start making things better or what course of action to take.

Source 3 Asher, 17

When I found out I was pregnant I was terrified. My mum got over it really quickly and is supportive. But my dad didn't talk to me for ages. He really disapproves of what I've done. He wants me to have the baby adopted. He says we can't afford another mouth to feed. He's lost his job and money is tight. If he's at home all day why can't he look after the baby while Mum is at work and I'm at school?

Source 4 Ruby, 16

As I walk home from school every day, I think about how my life has changed since my mum and dad split up. My mother recently re-married and while I see my dad once a month (he lives a long way away), I really miss him. My stepdad has his own children who I get on with OK, but I feel that he is always putting them ahead of me and doesn't treat us equally. I have spoken to Mum about this, but she just says that I am imagining it – I think about this a lot and don't feel as happy as I once did.

Source 5 Sierra, 15

Activity 2

Problem-solving

Read Sources 3–5 and consider the different challenges each person is facing. Which of the approaches in Sources 1–2 would help them to manage the situation and their feelings surrounding it? Explain your reasons for each.

Activity 3

Facing future challenges

Reflect back to when you chose options in Year 9 – or forward to what you will do after your GCSEs. These were and will be big challenges and opportunities. In the next few months you are likely to face a challenge or two. What might these be and which of the strategies you have learned about would you use and why?

By the end of this lesson you will:
- identify your own stress triggers
- develop strategies to manage your time effectively
- reflect on your own school–life balance
- understand other people's attitude to work and personal happiness.

The phrase 'work–life balance' has become quite common. One way of explaining this idea is to see it as balancing the amount of time you spend doing your job compared with the amount of time you spend with your family and doing things you enjoy.

Achieving the right work–life balance may sound like something that will affect you in the future. However, although right now you may not be holding down full-time jobs, you may still feel under a lot of pressure from daily responsibilities. Everyone can benefit from finding a healthy balance rather than having a life that feels like a juggling act. Could managing our time more efficiently be a key way to achieve better mental health? (See Source 1.)

Prioritising – time management for students

When there seems to be a million things to do, prioritising can seem difficult. It is important to look at which activities or projects will take longest, which are hardest and which are due or are happening soonest.

- Work out a balance between school and other activities that makes sense for you, and set an amount of time for each activity.
- Make a list of what you have to do, and when you have to have it done.
- Cross out or check off what you have done.
- Decide how much time you want to spend on each item on your to-do list.
- Break up bigger projects into more manageable parts, for example, with an assignment, you can start with finding sources, then taking notes, then doing an outline, writing a rough draft and then editing and proofreading. This way, you don't have to do it all at once.
- Plan what times you want to set aside for work, and what time you have for other activities (study after breakfast, take a break for lunch, play a sport for one hour, study until dinner, then relax for the night and get a good night's sleep so you can focus the next day).

Source: Palo Alto Medical Foundation for Health Care, Research and Education

Source 1

Starter

It's such a hassle!

In a survey, 124 teenagers were asked to talk about what stressed them the most. The topics they came up with (in alphabetical order) were:
- family/parents
- managing time
- school/homework
- social life
- sports.

Which of these do you think was mentioned most and which least? Put the five in the order you think they occurred – from most to least mentioned as the main source of stress.

Activity 1

Work–life balance

What strategies would you recommend to a friend who felt stressed or overwhelmed when trying to manage their time and commitments? Use Source 1 to help you.

Activity 2

Finding out more

Some people spend so much time working, they don't notice that they're missing out on time for themselves and people who matter to them.

1 Use the quiz in Source 2 to interview three other people at school. It will help them identify how healthy their school–life balance is.

2 Feed back your findings to the class and then discuss the following questions:

   a Did you spot any common factors or experiences amongst people who felt they had a good school–life balance?

   b People can get very excited, passionate and involved in school – but can this hurt the rest of their lives in any way?

   c Should one live to work, or work to live?

Activity 3

Dividing my time

Here are five things that can compete for your time:
- family
- me-time
- education/school
- friends/social life
- sports.

Do you balance your time evenly? Can you think of anything else not listed above that impacts on your school–life balance?

A school–life quiz

1 When you are not actually at school or travelling to it, how often do you think or worry about school?

   a I don't
   b Not very often
   c Once a week
   d Most days
   e It's always on my mind

2 How many hours a week do you spend doing homework?

   a Less than 10
   b 11–13
   c 14–16
   d 17–19
   e More than 20

3 How often do you make sure you have at least 1 hour to do things non-school related?

   a Every day
   b Most days
   c Once a week
   d Only if I'm able to
   e My own time? What's that?

4 How often does pressure of school stop you enjoying time with your family or friends?

   a Never! Family comes first
   b Not very often
   c More often than I would like
   d All the time
   e Friends? There's no time for friends.

5 Does school ever have a negative effect on the rest of your life?

   a No – it's only school
   b Not very often
   c Often
   d All the time
   e I have no life outside school

6 Do you ever feel tired or sad because of school?

   a No – it's only school
   b Not very often
   c Often
   d All the time
   e Too tired to be sad

7 Does school ever make you feel worried, anxious or upset?

   a No – it's only school
   b Not very often
   c Often
   d All the time
   e No time to be anxious

Mostly (a) and (b): You have a fair school–life balance – remember as exams approach this may change as you prepare;

Mostly (b) and (c): You are not doing badly – but make sure you keep some time for yourself;

Mostly (c) and (d): You need to look at your school–life balance in some areas;

Mostly (d) and (e): You need help in sorting out your school–life balance.

Source 2

By the end of this lesson you will:

- know about the number of people affected by bereavement
- be able to explain the five stages of grief
- be able to explain different ways people cope with bereavement
- understand how to support those who have suffered bereavements.

Starter

Early experiences

We can feel loss in several situations. Identify times when you might feel loss and discuss them with a partner.

Sooner or later in life, each of us will probably experience bereavement and grief.

Being bereaved usually means that someone we love has died. When this happens people go through all sorts of changes that may affect them emotionally, physically, spiritually and socially. The impact on each person will be different – but most people will feel enormous pain or sorrow, and learning to live with loss may take years. Each year it is estimated that in the UK:

- 20,000 children and young people under the age of 16 are bereaved of a parent
- 182,500 women become widows
- 175,000 men become widowers
- 12,000 children die.

Activity 1

Marking a bereavement

The photos in Source 1 show different funeral rituals. Discuss why people feel the need to have such funeral rituals around the death of someone or something they love.

Military funeral

Headstone of a grave in a Jewish cemetery – the stones are placed by visitors who remember the dead person

Burying a dead pet

Source 1 People will choose to mark death in different ways ...

The grief cycle

Grief is the process people go through after a loss, and everyone grieves differently. The grief cycle can help in understanding and accepting feelings, but you may move between stages more than once, and in different orders – the amount of time this takes will be different for everyone. Your culture and upbringing may also affect how you grieve.

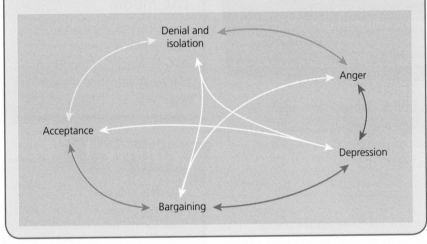

Source 2

Different people express their grief in different ways. Eric Clapton, guitarist and singer-songwriter, expressed his grief at the loss of his child by writing the song 'Tears in Heaven'.

Activity 2

Adjustment

'Life will never be the same. It's different. And that's OK.'

These are the words of someone who has experienced bereavement. Look at Source 2. How does it help to explain the feelings this person is going through?

Activity 3

Expressing feelings

Look up the lyrics of 'Tears in Heaven', especially lines 5–8. How do you interpret what Eric Clapton was trying to say?

Activity 4

Helping others to cope with bereavement

Some people find it difficult to know what to say when someone dies. They might be unintentionally thoughtless or unkind. Perhaps they just don't understand, are frightened or unaware. In groups, produce a short role play designed to help someone support a friend who is bereaved.

1   Research and decide what you would include and the language you would use to help support your friend. Use the websites listed below as a starting point:
   * www.hopeagain.org.uk/hope-again-talking-about-it
   * https://help2makesense.org/3-ways-to-support-a-grieving-friend/
   * www.childline.org.uk/info-advice/your-feelings/feelings-emotions/when-someone-dies/#waystocopewhensomeonedies
2   Create your role play.

Activity 5

Here and now

Sometimes when a loved one has died people say, 'I wish I'd told them how much they meant to me'. Choose someone alive now who you really like or care about. Create a one-line appreciation message to give them.

By the end of this lesson you will:

- evaluate the effectiveness of media campaigns in promoting health
- be able to give examples of how social marketing is used in health campaigns
- develop your own ideas to promote a health issue.

The media can play a valuable role in bringing important issues to our attention. This is particularly the case when it comes to health, where the media are used by the government to make people aware of health issues and to try and influence behaviour.

Social marketing

The way that governments have communicated messages about public health changed during the twentieth century from using simple 'finger-wagging' slogans such as 'Don't litter' and 'Stop smoking' to using social marketing techniques to persuade people to change their behaviour, and engage them with the message.

Social marketing is where adverts and marketing messages are designed to influence behaviours – not to benefit the advertiser, but to benefit the person being targeted by the campaign and society in general.

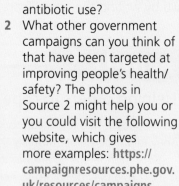

Source 1 The Antibiotic Guardian pledge initiative, part of the national Keep Antibiotics Working campaign

Activity 1

Media health campaigns

1 Look at Source 1. Why do you think the Keep Antibiotics Working campaign was so successful in raising awareness about the need to reduce antibiotic use?

2 What other government campaigns can you think of that have been targeted at improving people's health/safety? The photos in Source 2 might help you or you could visit the following website, which gives more examples: **https://campaignresources.phe.gov.uk/resources/campaigns**

3 Are there any that are targeted particularly at young people? If so, how?

4 Imagine that the government makes a decision that there will only be *one* public health campaign per year aimed at young people of your age. What health message should that campaign convey in the twelve months starting today?

Public Health England (PHE) have stated that 5000 people per year die because of antibiotic resistance. Since 2017, the Keep Antibiotics Working campaign has aimed to highlight the risk of taking antibiotics when you don't need them.

As part of the campaign, TV adverts featuring antibiotic pills singing 'Every time you feel a bit under the weather, don't always think that we can make you better' have been broadcast to urge people to stop asking doctors and other healthcare professionals for antibiotics. As a further step individuals are invited to choose a pledge on the Antibiotic Guardian website about how they can contribute to helping Keep Antibiotics Working (Source 1).

Antibiotic resistance is perhaps one of the most significant global crises humans face, and unless we are able to reduce their use considerably or develop new antibiotics, then we may find that common infections, injuries and routine operations become much riskier.

The Keep Antibiotics Working campaign and the Change4Life (Source 3) campaign have used a variety of media to convey their messages, including radio, TV, social media, poster and leaflet campaigns.

Accessibility and language

Accessibility is vital with any health campaign. If the campaign isn't seen or heard by the target audience then it can't be effective. Social media has increased access to the target audience through platforms such as Twitter, Instagram and WhatsApp. Video bloggers (Vloggers) are also making use of social media platforms to share their knowledge with viewers, informing them about health issues, from diet through to STIs (Source 2). As the audience, it is important to be discerning when accessing such media. The internet currently has over 644 million active websites, and platforms such as Twitter receive over 500 million tweets per day. Although not all of these relate to health, a very high number do and so it is important to separate high quality and useful information from poor quality and unhelpful information. A survey for the UK Digital Health Report, based on 61 million Google searches and a survey of 1013 adults, found that a quarter of the people in the UK use the internet to self-diagnose conditions, often from websites or forums where contributors have little or no medical experience.

Another important consideration when devising a health campaign is the language used. It could be used to shock, such as 'Dying to take the call?' (an advert against using a mobile phone while driving), or words can be chosen carefully to promote positive responses. The Liverpool Schools Parliament proposed banning the word 'obesity' in their health campaigns and using the term 'unhealthy weight' instead. This is because they think the word obesity puts young people off confronting their weight problems.

In addition to the role social media can play in making us aware of health issues, there are also approximately 375 000 health apps available which claim to help improve our health. But do they work?

Source 2 An example of social marketing

Source 3 The Change4Life campaign is an example of social marketing

Some social marketing techniques

1 Celebrity endorsement – a well-known person says or shows how good something is.

2 Voice of authority/scientific evidence – experts (for example, doctors/scientists) use facts, statistics and research evidence to convince the target audience.

3 Band-wagon appeal – implies that because everyone is doing it then you should too.

4 Romance/sex appeal – very attractive people and situations are used to gain your attention and influence you.

5 Popularity appeal – suggests that if you engage with this you will become more popular.

6 Humour – making someone laugh is an effective way of engaging them and makes the issue more memorable/acceptable.

7 Distaste – startling, unusual or unpleasant image to gain your attention.

Source 4

Fancy a Becks?

Celebrities like David Beckham and Mila Kunis are being used by companies trading in alcoholic products, including whisky, to market their products and promote sales. Young people see these adverts on billboards, TV and in magazines and are also made aware of celebrity-endorsed alcoholic beverages through social media, sport and sponsorship. Research shows that this can lead to an increased chance of 'higher risk drinking'.

Furthermore, young people who buy branded alcohol merchandise, for example, clothing, are more likely to begin drinking.

Source: An article from *The Sun* newspaper, 14 March 2019

Source 5

Activity 3

Digital technology, social media and health marketing

1 Using the images in Sources 2 and 3 on the previous page and the information in Source 4, answer the following questions for each image:
  a What is the health issue?
  b What is the message?
  c What technique(s) are being used?
  d How effective do you think this example is in getting people to change their behaviour?

McDonald's came under fire for their 2019 Monopoly competition. It was branded a 'public health danger' because critics claimed it encouraged people to overeat. This seems particularly inappropriate when Britain's population faces increasing levels of obesity.

In order to enter the competition, in which customers could win prizes, cash and meals, customers had to purchase McDonald's food and drink to find out if they had won.

Source 6

Activity 4

Using positive language

1 Using the examples in Sources 2 and 3 (or one of the campaigns you looked at in Activity 1), how could you make the campaign positive rather than negative?
2 Outline a health/safety campaign using a positive approach.
  • Decide what health topic you want to draw attention to.
  • Decide on the age group you are aiming to reach.
  • Decide what important information/message you need to put across.
  • Decide the positive features of your campaign and why you think they will work better than a negative approach.

Activity 5

Discussion

Read through Sources 5 and 6. Do you feel the health campaigns such as those looked at in this lesson are outweighed by media and advertising promoting unhealthy products such as fast food and alcohol?

By the end of this lesson you will:
- be able to explain the risks about increasing levels of obesity in the UK
- reflect on your own diet and impact on your own health
- reflect on your own level of physical activity and the impact on your own health.

In 2018, Simon Stevens, the Chief Executive Officer for the NHS, announced that obesity was one of the biggest threats to health in the UK.

- 1 in 4 children enter primary school with a weight classed as overweight or obese.
- 1 in 3 children enter secondary school with a weight classed as overweight or obese.
- 50 per cent of all children will be overweight or obese by 2020.
- The UK is the most overweight country in Western Europe.
- 63 per cent of adults are classed as being overweight.
- Obesity increases the risk of some cancers, high blood pressure, heart disease, diabetes and stroke.
- Obesity is responsible for 30,000 deaths per year.
- The costs to the NHS are approximately £6.1 billion per year, which is expected to increase to £9.7 billion by 2050.
- The overall cost of obesity to wider society is estimated at £27 billion per year, which is expected to increase to £49 billion by 2050.

Source: adapted from NHS Digital, Statistics on Obesity, Physical Activity and Diet, England, 2019

Source 1 Obesity facts

You will no doubt be familiar with the concepts in Source 1. Most people you speak to will be aware of the link between an unhealthy lifestyle and risks to their health. So why do we do it? In many cases people will take more care of their phone or car than they do their own health.

A number of campaigns have promoted healthy eating. These include the government's '5 a day' and 'Change4Life' campaigns, and celebrity chefs such as Jamie Oliver promoting healthier food in schools. Despite all these efforts, the statistics in Source 1 suggest they aren't having the sustained impact they need.

Starter

Why do we do it?

Why, despite knowing the health risks of eating unhealthy food, smoking and drinking, do people still do it?

A better diet and more exercise are the two main aspects to improve if you want to become healthier.

Diet

Teenagers need lots of energy as they are still growing. The amount of energy that food and drink contain is measured in kilojoules (kJ) and kilocalories (kcal), usually referred to as calories.

The NHS website recommendations are outlined in Source 2.

Age	Boys	Girls
13	10,100kJ/2,414kcal	9,300kJ/2,223kcal
14	11,000kJ/2,629kcal	9,800kJ/2,342kcal
15	11,800kJ/2,820kcal	10,000kJ/2,390kcal
16	12,400kJ/2,964kcal	10,100kJ/2,414kcal
17	12,900kJ/3,083kcal	10,300kJ/2,462kcal
18	13,200kJ/3,155kcal	10,300kJ/2,462kcal

Source 2

These recommendations are only a guide as teenagers may need more or less energy depending on how physically active they are.

Equally important to the number of calories is the type of food that is eaten. Advice from the NHS is shown in Source 3.

Activity 1

My meal plan

Research a number of healthy breakfast, lunch and dinner options that a teenager could eat to meet the recommended daily calorie intake in Source 2.

A healthy, balanced diet for teenagers should include:

- at least 5 portions of a variety of fruit and vegetables every day
- meals based on starchy foods, such as potatoes, bread, pasta and rice – choose wholegrain varieties when possible
- some milk and dairy products – choose low-fat options where you can
- some foods that are good sources of protein – such as meat, fish, eggs, beans and lentils.

Teenagers shouldn't fill up on too many sugary or fatty foods – such as crisps, sweets, cakes, biscuits – or sugary fizzy drinks. These tend to be high in calories but contain few nutrients.

Source 3

Exercise

We are all aware of the benefits of regular exercise.

To stay healthy or to improve health, young people need to do three types of physical activity each week:

- aerobic exercise
- exercises to strengthen their bones
- exercises to strengthen their muscles.

To maintain a basic level of health, children and young people aged 5 to 18 need to do:

- at least 60 minutes of physical activity every day – this should range from moderate activity, such as cycling and playground activities, to vigorous activity, such as running and tennis
- on three days a week, these activities should involve exercises for strong muscles and bones, such as swinging on playground equipment, hopping and skipping and sports such as gymnastics or tennis.

Children and young people should also reduce the time they spend sitting for extended periods of time, including watching TV, playing computer games and travelling by car when they could walk or cycle.

Being active for at least 60 minutes a day is linked to better general health, stronger bones and muscles and higher levels of self-esteem.

Source 4

Phones v sports

A study from San Diego University which used data from over one million teenagers, found that those who spent more time on social media, gaming, texting and video-chatting on their phones were not as happy as those who played sports, went outside and interacted with real human beings.

The findings suggest that it is the phone use itself that contributes to making teenagers unhappy, not just what they are looking at. Teenagers that spend four or five hours a day on their phones increased the risk factor of suicide by 71 per cent.

Those that took part in regular sport or other physical activity were much more likely to feel happy about themselves and life in general.

The report suggested that teenagers should not spend more than two hours per day on digital media and should take part in more exercise, and hang out with friends face-to-face.

While the San Diego study suggests a link between phone use and happiness, a study by Oxford University in 2019 contradicts this, stating that even before bedtime, being online, gaming or watching TV is not damaging to young people's mental health.

Source 5

Activity 2

Enough exercise?

1 Why do you think it can be difficult for teenagers to meet the recommended physical activity guidance from the NHS?
2 Research local clubs, sports centres or online fitness coaches. Produce a poster, information leaflet or vlog/instastory for teenagers covering the following:
- the importance of physical activity
- the amount of physical activity that teenagers should be doing
- examples of physical activity that can help maintain a person's health
- local clubs, sports centres or online coaches that could be used.

Activity 3

Does screen time really affect health?

In pairs, make a list of the positives and negatives on a person's health from using mobile technology.

Activity 4

Self-reflection

Having read through the sources in this topic, do you feel that you eat healthily enough and take part in enough physical exercise? How could you improve your own situation?

By the end of the lesson you will:

- be able to explain why it is important for individuals to take responsibility for their own health
- know how to check your own body
- be able to explain what is involved in health screening and where to seek advice.

Starter

I know I shouldn't!

Name three things you do that you know are unhealthy – why do you do them?

Source 1 Health is a whole-person issue

Look at Source 1. Health includes more than just the physical body – it is also about the mind and the spirit. It is our mental health and the emotions we experience, along with the physical body, which make up the whole person.

There are many things that contribute to making us healthy and keeping us healthy. Some examples are listed in Source 2.

a) 5-a-day fruit and vegetables	b) Walking instead of driving/using the bus	c) A good night's sleep
d) Using the stairs instead of the lift	e) Being able to talk about loss and death	f) Not bottling things up
g) Laughing when you can	h) Access to local healthcare	i) Having interests, hobbies and pastimes
j) A balanced approach to eating	k) Being alcohol aware – and drinking in moderation	l) 30 active minutes five times a week, e.g. swimming, rollerblading, active play, etc.
m) Relaxation – time to chill	n) Going smoke free	o) Feeling loved and loving others

Source 2 Parts of a healthy lifestyle

Activity 1

Valuing your health

1 Look at Source 2. Which of the three categories of mind, body and spirit would you place each of these under? Can some of them be placed in more than one category?

2 Draw a health pyramid as shown. Put the different ways to good health listed in Source 2 into your health pyramid, making a decision on where each should go. Note that you have 15 ideas but only 10 spaces on your pyramid. Think carefully about which you will choose. Be ready to explain your choices.

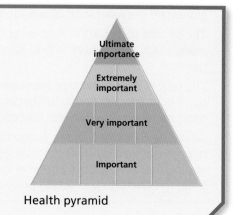

Health pyramid

In addition to looking after our own physical and mental health through healthy eating and exercise, we also need to be looking for signs or symptoms that we might have something wrong.

When you were young you will have most likely been given a number of vaccinations to stop you getting particular illnesses.

In addition to those in Source 3, there are also a number of optional vaccinations available including chickenpox and tuberculosis.

The vaccines in Source 3 are usually given to you as a child. This means that it is your parents who decide whether you have the vaccine or not, just as they are most likely to decide what you will be eating and how much time you spend on your phone and so on. As you become older, it is important that you take responsibility for your own health.

One important aspect of being health aware is knowing your own body. As a teenager you are going through lots of changes, most of which are perfectly normal. However, every now and again you may have concerns as something may not seem right. If you ever have any concerns you should make an appointment with your doctor (GP).

As you get older, it is important to check your body (self-examination) regularly or attend screening services which can help detect possible illness. The NHS give the advice shown in Source 4 and 5.

Vaccination	When given
HPV vaccine (girls only)	12–13 years of age
3 in 1 teenage booster – tetanus, diphtheria and polio	14 years of age
MenACWY vaccine (meningitis)	14 years of age and new university students age 19–25

Source 3 NHS timeline of teenage vaccinations

Activity 2

Do it now!

By now you'll appreciate that you are going through a stage in your life that will affect your future. This is especially true now while your intellectual and physical skills are still developing. What healthy habits can a teenager realistically develop now to help them optimise their future health?

Activity 3

What are they?

You may be familiar with some of the names of the illnesses in Source 3, but do you know what the symptoms are? With a partner, research those that you are not sure about and find the symptoms.

Checking your testicles

Most men's testicles are about the same size, though it's common for one to be slightly bigger than the other. It's also common for one testicle to hang lower than the other.

The testicles should feel smooth, without any lumps or bumps, and firm but not hard. You may feel a soft tube at the back of each testicle, which is called the epididymis.

If you notice any changes or anything unusual about your testicles, you should see your GP.

What causes lumps and swelling in the testicles?

There are several causes of testicular lumps and swellings:

- **varicocele** – caused by enlarged veins in the testicles (may look like a bag of worms)

- **hydrocele** – a swelling caused by fluid around the testicle

- **epididymal cyst** – a lump caused by a collection of fluid in the epididymis

- **testicular torsion** – a sudden painful swelling that occurs when a testicle becomes twisted (this is a medical emergency and requires surgery as soon as possible)

- **epididymitis** – a chlamydia infection in the epididymis can cause inflammation, swelling and tenderness inside the scrotum (ball sack); a few men will notice that the whole of the scrotum is red and tender (this is called epididymo-orchitis)

- **testicular cancer** – an estimated 4 in 100 lumps are cancer, so this is an uncommon cause of lumps.

What are the signs of testicular cancer?

The early signs of testicular cancer are easy to spot. Look out for one or more of the following:

- a hard lump on the front or side of a testicle
- swelling or enlargement of a testicle
- an increase in firmness of a testicle

- pain or discomfort in a testicle or in the scrotum (the sac that holds the testicles)
- an unusual difference between one testicle and the other.

If you find a lump or swelling, or any of the above signs, it's important to get it checked out by your doctor.

Source: from www.nhs.co.uk

Source 4

Checking your breasts

There's no right or wrong way to check your breasts. But it is important to know how your breasts usually look and feel. That way, you can spot any changes quickly and report them to your GP.

Be breast aware

Every woman's breasts are different in terms of size, shape and consistency. It's also possible for one breast to be larger than the other.

Get used to how your breasts feel at different times of the month. This can change during your menstrual cycle. For example, some women have tender and lumpy breasts, especially near the armpit, around the time of their period.

After the menopause, normal breasts feel softer, less firm and not as lumpy.

The NHS Breast Screening Programme has produced a 5-point plan for being breast aware:

- know what's normal for you
- look at your breasts and feel them
- know what changes to look for
- report any changes without delay
- attend routine screening if you're 50 or over.

Look at your breasts and feel each breast and armpit, and up to your collarbone. You may find it easiest to do this in the shower or bath, by running a soapy hand over each breast and up under each armpit.

You can also look at your breasts in the mirror. Look with your arms by your side and also with them raised.

Changes to look out for

See your GP if you notice any of the following changes:

- a change in the size, outline or shape of your breast
- a change in the look or feel of your skin, such as puckering or dimpling
- a new lump, thickening or bumpy area in one breast or armpit that is different from the same area on the other side
- nipple discharge that's not milky
- bleeding from your nipple
- a moist, red area on your nipple that doesn't heal easily
- any change in nipple position, such as your nipple being pulled in or pointing differently
- a rash on or around your nipple
- any discomfort or pain in one breast, particularly if it's a new pain and doesn't go away (although pain is only a symptom of breast cancer in rare cases).

Always see your GP if you are concerned

Changes can happen for many reasons, and most of them aren't serious. Lots of women have breast lumps, and 9 out of 10 are not cancerous.

However, if you find changes in your breast that aren't normal for you, it's best to see your GP as soon as possible. This is because it is important to rule out breast cancer. If cancer is detected, then appropriate treatment should be planned as quickly as possible.

Source: www.nhs.co.uk

Source 5

NHS Digital

Breast Screening Programme, England 2017-18

Screening is intended to detect breast cancer at an early stage when there is a better chance of successful treatment. Women between the ages of 50 and 70 years are invited for regular breast screening (every three years) under a national programme.

Some women outside this age group are also screened as part of the NHS Breast Screening Programme, either through self or General Practitioner (GP) referral where appropriate, or as part of a research trial.

Uptake of invites

70.5%
took up invitation
(aged 50-70)

 72.1 71.1 70.5 ↓0.6% since 2016-17

Cancer detection

18,001
women (aged 45+) had cancers detected

8.4 cases per 1,000 screened

Types of cancer detected

78.6%
women (aged 45+) with cancer detected had invasive cancers[1]

1 One which has spread beyond the layer of tissue in which it developed and is growing into surrounding, healthy tissues.

Types of cancer detected

7,223
women (aged 45+) had invasive but small cancers[2]

2 Less than 15mm in diameter, usually too small to detect by hand.

Information and technology for better health and care

Read the full report: digital.nhs.uk/pubs/brstscreen1718

Source 6 The NHS's breast screening programme

Activity 4

Screening

The NHS also offer a number of 'screening services' to detect illness or a person's risk of illness.

1 Research the different screening services offered by the NHS. Use the website **https://www.nhs.uk/conditions/nhs-screening/** in addition to Sources 4, 5, 6 and 7.

2 Design a radio or TV advert to encourage a particular target audience to get checked. Source 6 provides some statistics from the NHS which you could use to demonstrate the importance of screening. Think about the work you did earlier in this chapter about the use of social media and marketing and so on.

Activity 5

Do we talk about it enough?

Do you regularly talk about health issues with your family and friends? If not, why not?

Oral health and visiting the dentist

At your check-up, your dentist will assess your current oral health, any risk of future disease and advise you on the care and treatment required to secure good oral health. It is important that you try to keep your teeth healthy and clean to maintain good oral health.

What will happen at your check-up?

At your check-up, your dentist may:

- carry out a full examination of your mouth, teeth and gums

- ask about your general health and any problems you have had with your teeth, mouth or gums since your last visit

- ask about and give advice on your diet, smoking and drinking

- ask about your teeth-cleaning habits and give you advice on the most appropriate ways to keep your mouth, teeth and gums healthy

- explain any risks, as well as dental costs, of all treatment you may need

- discuss with you when your next visit should be.

Many of us have got used to going to the dentist every six months but you might need to go more often or less often than this depending on how healthy your mouth and teeth are. Your dentist should talk to you about when you should have your next appointment.

Source: from www.nhs.co.uk

Source 7

By the end of this lesson you will:

- know what positive and negative risks are
- know what is meant by 'heart' and 'head' responses to risk
- evaluate your own personal responses to risk and risk-taking
- be able to explain how and why people perceive risks differently.

As a teenager, you are not just growing physically but you are also developing mentally – both your physical brain and your emotions/thought processes (see Source 1). Developing a healthy pattern to your lifestyle now will help you maximise your future potential.

As the UK law stands, you are considered to be a mature adult when you turn 18. However, according to brain scientists, people don't become fully adult until they reach their thirties - and they also claim that the age at which adulthood is reached differs for everyone.

Research also suggests that people aged 18 are still experiencing brain changes which can affect their behaviour. These changes can also make them more likely to develop mental health disorders.

Source 1

Starter

Do it now!

By now you'll appreciate that you are going through a stage in your life that will affect your future. This is especially true now while your intellectual and physical skills are still developing, which can affect the decisions you make and the risks you take (see Source 1).

What risks do you take? Think about things you do every day such as crossing the road and those that may be less obvious. How do you decide whether or not to take the risk?

Research shows that teenagers and young adults take more risks than any other age group. This may include dangerous driving, drug use and sexual behaviour. Even though teenagers are educated about such topics they often continue to engage in risky behaviour.

There are three main reasons for this:

1   Brain imaging studies have shown that there are some areas of the teenage brain that are influenced more readily by peer relationships than are adults. This suggests that the motivation behind teenage decisions is often peer focused.

2   Teenagers are more distressed when they are excluded by their peers than adults. An area of the brain known as the right ventrolateral prefrontal cortex helps in coping with negative responses from peers by reducing distress. However, research shows that this part of the brain is used at a greater level by adults to cope with such situations, whereas teenagers are more likely to make a decision that pleases their peers to avoid being socially excluded and the distress that may follow.

3   Teenagers were found to use areas of the brain that are focused on rewards they receive from their peers, as the lateral prefrontal cortex that adults use to make decisions is not yet ready to assist them in mature self-regulation.

Activity 1

What's the buzz?

Look at Source 2. A young person is playing a computer game. Discuss the following questions:

1   Look at the expression on the young person's face. What words would you use to describe the 'buzz' they might be feeling?
2   Why are games like this so mesmerising?
3   Are there any risks or dangers associated with gaming?

Source 2 What's the buzz?

What is risk?

Every action that holds the possibility of a positive or negative outcome is a risk.

A **positive risk** is one where the intended outcome is beneficial to well-being, for example, sports, performing on stage, speaking in public, going for a job interview.

A **negative risk** is one where the undesired outcome damages wellbeing, for example, dependency on drugs and alcohol, carrying a weapon, exceeding the speed limit.

If you stop to think about it, every risk should involve weighing up:

■   the probability or likelihood of something happening
■   the impact or severity of the consequences.

Gambling

Gambling is an example of a risk-taking activity. People think of gambling in different ways but it usually involves:

- two or more people, usually an operator and an individual
- risking a stake, usually money, on the outcome of a future event
- paying the stake by the loser to the winner.

In simple terms, gambling is any behaviour that involves risking money or valuables on the outcome of a game, contest or other event. This event or game may be totally or in part dependent on chance.

Activity 2

Gambling is …

In Source 3 there are some questions about gambling. What are your thoughts? Discuss the questions in groups.

Gamblers are bad people?

Scratch cards encourage people to gamble?

Only idiots gamble?

Online gambling is a mug's game?

Gambling is a risk worth taking?

Slot machines are harmless?

Source 3 Do you believe that …

Gambling is one type of risk-taking activity that can have serious consequences. In the next activity you will have the chance to think about other activities that have risks attached.

Activity 3

Rate the risk

Rank the following activities from 'totally safe' to 'extremely risky'.
- bungee jumping
- carrying a knife for protection
- drinking a bottle of spirits
- having unprotected sex
- playing fruit machines
- smoking cigarettes
- speaking in front of a group
- talking in internet chat rooms.

We are all individuals and have different attitudes to risk-taking. What for some of us might be a positive risk-taking experience, might feel very negative and unsettling for others. We also have different attitudes to weighing up risks: some people will be very thoughtful and others will just jump in.

Activity 4

Thinking about you

1 a What is the biggest negative risk you've ever taken?
   b Did you do anything to limit the potential for harm?
2 a What's the biggest positive risk you've ever taken?
   b What did you gain from taking it?
3 a Looking to the future, what positive risk would you most like to take?
   b What might stop you from taking that risk?
   c What would you gain from taking that risk?
4 On a scale of 1–10, how big a risk-taker would you say you are (with 1 as mega safe!)?

Activity 5

Obsessed?

Look at the young person in Source 4. If you are experiencing strong emotions (pleasure, fear, a buzz and so on), does that make it harder or easier to weigh up the risks in any situation? Explain your answer.

Source 4

By the end of this lesson you will:

- be able to explain how online activity leaves 'online footprints'
- be able to explain the importance of being responsible online
- evaluate your own online behaviour
- understand how irresponsible online behaviour could affect future prospects.

In August 2018, Tim Berners-Lee, the man who invented the World Wide Web, gave an interview to *Vanity Fair*. In this interview he stated that he was 'devastated' with the way the internet had been used for everything from fake news to mass surveillance.

Starter

Misuse of the internet

Why do you think Tim Berners-Lee felt 'devastated' about his invention?

Source 1 Tim Berners-Lee

The average person in the UK now spends an average of one day per week using the internet, whether it is using social media, watching a film or buying groceries.

You will have grown up with the internet being common place, but you may have heard your parents or carers say things such as 'I remember when children used to go out and play' or 'I used to listen to the charts and record them off the radio', as they will remember a time when life was different.

The speed of the change that has taken place has been extremely quick, and in many cases the authorities and regulating bodies have struggled to keep up.

Activity 1

Legal ages

Source 2 has a number of apps that have been given age ratings, some of which you may have used while underage. In pairs, discuss whether or not you feel it is acceptable to use these if you are younger than the age rating requires.

WhatsApp: age rating 13 — **13**

Snapchat: age rating 13 — **13**

Tinder: age rating 18 — **18**

Instagram: age rating 13 — **13**

Source 2 Age rating

The use of the internet, associated apps and technology are a right that we all now have, but as with any right, there is also a responsibility such as not to post inappropriate comments or pictures which could cause offence to others. Any online activity is stored for approximately a year and is referred to as your 'online footprint'.

Despite precautions that you may take, someone, for example, your internet service provider (ISP) will be able to see everything you do online. While there are steps you can take, such as cleaning up your browser history, using a privacy mode or using a virtual private network (VPN), someone, somewhere will still have a record of the websites you have visited and any online activity (including mobile apps and so on). Should the need arise, such as for a criminal or terror-related investigation, this information could be requested.

Most websites or apps ask you to agree to certain terms and conditions, of which there are so many that most people just tick the agree box. However, by doing so you are allowing your details to be shared with other companies, as Source 3 details.

Activity 2

Future prospects

In groups, read through one of the Sources 3–6. Answer the questions that follow as a group and be prepared to share your answers with the other groups.
1   How could a person's life be affected by their online behaviour:
    a   in the short term?
    b   in the long term?
2   Reflect on your own social media postings. Have you ever posted anything that you now regret? What impact could this have on you personally? Discuss your thoughts among your group.

I'm A Celeb's Jack Maynard issues apology for deleted 2011 tweet about rape

Former I'm A Celebrity camp mate and YouTube star Jack Maynard has issued a second Twitter apology after an historical tweet in which he joked about rape came to light.

The Sun reported that in a deleted tweet from 2011 a 16-year-old Maynard had joked that if his fans could get him to 1500 Twitter followers he would 'kiss you … most likely rape you though'.

'I have taken some time to reflect on the comments, tweets and ultimately my behaviour in the past, including a tweet [sent] in 2011 that is the subject of a story today,' he wrote on Twitter.

'I was young, naive and stupid – but as I said previously, age is no excuse. My immaturity meant that I didn't stop for a second to think whether these comments would hurt or harm anyone – something I have learnt is entirely wrong.'

He continued, 'If I had just thought for a moment, about how stupid they are I would never have said them. Nothing can justify the language I used, there is no defence – I am truly sorry. My childish attitude back then is not a representation of my thoughts and feelings now'.

Source: Radio Times, 2017

Source 3

Man jailed for four months over Facebook threat to kill MP

Mark Sands told Caroline Ansell he would 'personally come round to your house and stab you to death'

A factory worker has been jailed for four months for posting on Facebook a 'sinister and menacing' threat to stab a Conservative MP to death.

Mark Sands, 51, was sentenced at Brighton magistrates court having previously pleaded guilty to a charge of 'sending via electronic communications a message that was grossly offensive' to the Eastbourne and Willingdon MP Caroline Ansell.

The court was told that Sands wrote: 'If you vote to take £30 off my money, I will personally come round to your house … and stab you to death.'

On his Facebook profile under the heading work, Sands wrote: 'The Killing Fields, Trainee Murderer.' Under political views, he had 'Kill your local MP'.

He also posted other messages including 'End poverty, kill a Tory now.' A picture of the murdered Labour MP Jo Cox also featured on his page with the words 'sawn-off 2.2'.

Source: *The Guardian*, 12 April 2017

Source 4

A report by findlaw.com highlights the concerns about the things young people are posting online and the impact they could have on their future and career opportunities. The report which focused on 18-34 year olds found that …

- 29 per cent of respondents had posted a tweet, update, photo or other post that they were worried a potential employer could see.

- 21 per cent of respondents deleted posts they had made due to worries about problems they may cause at work.

Removing such comments and posts that people had concerns about in the survey may not be as simple as many think. Although you may remove a post from your own account, it may already be elsewhere on the internet. With this in mind it is best to assume that anything you post online, could be there forever – so post carefully.

Source 5

Posting inappropriate comments on social media could have a negative impact on your career prospects. A survey in 2018 by CareerBuilder, highlighted that 70 per cent of potential employers screen social media during the recruitment process, while 43 per cent used it to monitor current staff.

There are a number of reasons for looking at social media but when looking to recruit a new member of staff, employers need to make sure they have the person that will fit best with their business.

Source 6

Activity 3

The right to be forgotten

What is the 'Right to be forgotten'? Research what it is and the process to achieve it.

Activity 4

Is it appropriate?

As a child, your parents or carers will have no doubt taken lots of pictures of you and in many cases posted them on social media. Is it appropriate for parents or carers to post pictures of their children on social media sites?

By the end of this lesson you will:
- be able to describe what cyberbullying is and how it affects people
- be able to describe what trolling is and how it affects people
- understand how and why hacking occurs and know how to protect yourself online
- know how to address and report online concerns.

Starter

Internet pros and cons

1 Make a list of all the positive things the internet and social media can be used for. For example, sharing of photos with family and friends.
2 Make a list of all the negative things the internet and social media can be used for. For example, grooming.

Used in the right way, the internet and social media provide exciting opportunities for us all.

Despite the benefits, it is important to be aware of the problems that can occur when online and how to deal with them if they arise.

Cyberbullying

The NSPCC define bullying and cyberbullying as:

> Bullying: behaviour that hurts someone else. It includes name calling, hitting, pushing, spreading rumours, threatening or undermining someone. It can happen anywhere – at school, at home or online. It's usually repeated over a long period of time and can hurt a child both physically and emotionally.
>
> Cyberbullying: bullying that takes place online. Unlike bullying in the real world, online bullying can follow a child wherever they go, via social networks, gaming and mobile phone.

Technology gives potential bullies another platform to harass, threaten and target others. Sometimes cyberbullying may be easy to spot, for example, a tweet, text or response to an online status that is unpleasant. On other occasions it may be less obvious, for example, posting personal information, photos or other media online to upset or embarrass someone. Fake accounts or online profiles may even be created with the sole intention of upsetting, victimising and bullying.

In some cases cyberbullying could be accidental. As messages via email, text and apps are impersonal, it is difficult to detect the tone, so what may be meant as a joke could be taken the wrong way. However, a repeated pattern of hurtful messages is unlikely to be an accident.

Cyberbullying can include:
- sending threatening or abusive text messages
- creating and sharing embarrassing images or videos
- trolling – the sending of menacing or upsetting messages on social networks, chat rooms or online games
- excluding children from online games, activities or friendship groups
- shaming someone online
- setting up hate sites or groups about a particular child
- encouraging young people to self-harm
- voting for or against someone in an abusive poll
- creating fake accounts, hijacking or stealing online identities to embarrass a young person or cause trouble using their name
- sending explicit messages, also known as sexting
- pressuring children into sending sexual images or engaging in sexual conversations.

Source 1 Types of cyberbullying

Activity 1

Dealing with cyberbullies and trolls

Sources 1–2 provide examples of what cyberbullying and trolling are, the impacts they can have and the possible consequences for those involved. Using this information and your own research, prepare an assembly, presentation, web article or leaflet to give to younger students in the school that provides information about what to do if they are a victim of cyberbullying or trolling. You should include the following:
- What it is.
- The effects it can have on those being targeted.
- How they can stop it happening, including the ideas below:
  - steps to take, for example, use the mute option on Twitter
  - organisations that support with cyberbullying and trolling
  - how to report any concerns, for example, to Twitter
  - advice about managing your online profile and security
  - talking to a trusted adult, for example, a teacher or parent/carer.

Trolling

People will often make comments online to or about someone that they wouldn't say directly face-to-face. In many cases comments may be made to someone the person doesn't know, or about an issue they don't really care about. They simply want to cause an argument or offence. An example of this is trolling.

The Oxford Dictionary defines 'trolling' as:

> **Making a deliberately offensive or provocative online post with the aim of upsetting someone or eliciting an angry response from them.**

The effects of trolling and cyberbullying

Fiona from Cardiff claims that social media 'trolls' have ruined her life, by superimposing her face onto pornographic images and sharing them online.

Comments left for Fiona told her to 'kill herself' and encouraged others to burgle her home after her address was shared on Twitter.

Fiona, 17, had open profiles on a number of social media sites including Twitter, Instagram and Live.me with thousands of followers.

She was repeatedly sent pornographic images and had pictures of her family home shared online with messages encouraging her to commit suicide.

The comments led Fiona to become depressed and she has since been prescribed anxiety tablets, and rarely leaves home as her confidence and self-esteem is so low. 'I am worried that I could hear the same comments whilst I am out if I am recognised. This has ruined my life.'

Source 2

Laws have been introduced to deal with internet trolls and the consequences for those convicted can be severe.

Another example of things going wrong online is 'hacking'. Hacking is the unauthorised access to a person's or business' data or computer system. Research suggests that a new hack is being implemented to businesses, organisations and individuals every 39 seconds.

In recent years there have been a number of high-profile data hacks including in 2018 when Instagram users were locked out of their accounts; however, it is estimated that 44 records/account details are stolen every second.

Hackers are always looking for new ways to hack people. It may be easy to spot a fake email asking you to click on a link, but when hackers are hiding their attacks in what may appear as an innocent social media post, it becomes more difficult. Sources 3 and 4 show the impact of hacks on individuals and organisations.

Instagram hack

Thousands of Instagram users have been permanently locked out of their accounts following reported 'hacks' originating in Russia.

Users have reported that profile pictures, usernames and 'bio' details have been altered, with the accounts then left unused, but in the control of the hackers, who can then decide what to do with them.

Paula from London said that 'the hackers have changed my linked email address, which effectively locks me out. I didn't receive any communication from Instagram telling me to change any of my security details and as a result my account is effectively useless. I'm not sure what the hackers intend to use the accounts for, but it is a little concerning.'

Reports of the hacking were first acknowledged a few weeks ago, and continue today, although no one is sure as to why the hackers want to take control of such a large number of Instagram accounts.

Instagram are investigating the reports of hacking and offering support to those that have been affected.

Source 3

Activity 2

Why hack?

What do you think the motives for a hacker could be?

Activity 3

Secure enough

How could a person improve their online security? Research online and make a step-by-step guide offering advice. You might find the following website useful: **https://www.cyberaware.gov.uk/**

Activity 4

Your own online security

Reflect on your own online security. Consider your research in Activity 3; do you think your online security is good enough?

School hacks

Some Year 11 students at a school in Bridport, Dorset, lost their GCSE coursework after hackers used ransomware to encrypt the school's files. Unfortunately, an email containing the virus was opened in error by a member of staff. It then infected the computer network where the work was saved.

Source 4

By the end of this lesson you will:

- be able to explain the reasons why people join gangs
- be able to explain the reasons why people carry knives
- be able to explain the potential consequences of being part of a gang or carrying a knife
- know where to seek advice and support if wanting to leave a gang.

A gang can be a group of mates or people that hang around together. You will probably have been part of a gang at some point in your life.

Unfortunately, the word 'gang' is more often than not associated with anti-social and criminal behaviour. You may be familiar with headlines such as those in Source 1.

Starter

We have all been in a gang

What is a gang? Have you ever been part of one?

Have we lost control of our streets?

Wild west London

How many more innocents must die?

11 stabbed to death in 16 days

Source 1

Bedfordshire Police define a gang as:

A gang is usually considered to be a group of people who spend time in public places that:

- see themselves (and are seen by others) as a noticeable group
- engage in a range of criminal activity and violence.

They may also have any or all of the following features:

- identify with or lay a claim over territory
- are in conflict with other, similar gangs.

However, if the majority of offending is of a lower, non-violent level then they would be considered a peer group and not a gang.

Activity 1

Why join a gang?

1 In pairs, make a list of reasons why you think a young person may join a gang. Be prepared to explain your ideas with the class.
2 What signs could indicate a young person is a member of a gang, for example, do they dress in a specific way?

Young people will join gangs for reasons that make sense to them.

Being part of a gang impacts the health and welfare of the individual in addition to that of their family, peers and community.

While gangs are often associated with boys, girls can also be affected although their involvement may be harder to spot. Girls may be asked to support gang members by hiding weapons or drugs, and be victims of emotional, physical and sexual abuse in acts of revenge or gang initiations.

Gang initiation

At the age of 11 Jasmine began a relationship with a boy she had liked for some time. He was part of a gang and for her to become a member she had to go through a number of initiation steps. These steps led to her spending time in prison as she participated in the kidnapping and rape of her friend.

Jasmine isn't proud of the things she did, but at the time she felt she had to take part as she wanted to be part of the gang 'family'. She has seen a number of her friends stabbed or shot in conflict with other gangs and, while knowing the dangers, continues to take part in criminal activity.

Source 2

Source 3 highlights how county line gangs (see page 39) are fuelling a rise in knife crime …

Gangs and knives

Vulnerable teenagers are being forced to carry drugs from London estates to the streets of Norwich.

A group of mothers in north London has been showing journalists the places where their sons have been forced to work in drug-dealing.

Sadly, the county lines system has led to a frightening increase in fatal stabbings. At the insistence of police chiefs, the government have pledged that they will take emergency action to deal with the matter.

Source 3

Knife crime

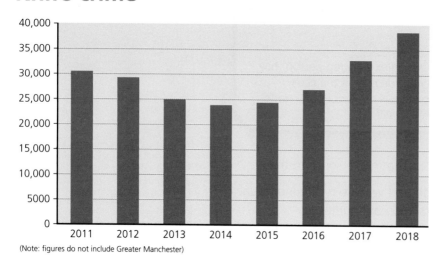

(Note: figures do not include Greater Manchester)

Source 4 Total knife offences in England and Wales.
Source: from the Office for National Statistics

One of the reasons for carrying a knife that might have come out of Activity 2 may have been 'protection'. You may have even carried or know someone that has carried a knife. By doing so a person is three times more likely to be stabbed themselves, often with the knife they took for protection in the first place.

Due to the increasing number of knife crimes and stabbings, there is a consistent call to make the sentences for those convicted tougher. The current sentencing rules are stated in Source 5.

Even though the consequences of carrying a knife may be known, and an individual may be uncomfortable in doing so, the expectation of others in the gang may override this. Leaving a gang isn't a straightforward process, and in many cases it may be important to seek professional advice.

Activity 3

Tough enough

1 Do you think the sentence guidelines for those carrying a knife are tough enough?
2 Question 1 asks you to reflect on the sentences given for carrying a knife if you are caught, but do you know what the law states about the buying and carrying of knives? Research the law about the buying and carrying of knives. You might find the following websites useful:

www.trusted2know.co.uk

www.gov.uk/buying-carrying-knives

Activity 2

Why carry a knife?

Why do you think people carry knives?

Consequences

There are minimum prison sentences in England and Wales for people aged 16 or over if they are found with a knife:

- which they are threatening to use to kill or harm another person
- in a public place or in a school and they have been previously convicted of possessing a weapon or threatening someone with a weapon.

In these circumstances:

- if aged 16 or 17, they will be sentenced to a detention and training order of at least 4 months
- if aged over 18, they will be sentenced to a minimum of 6 months/maximum of 4 years in custody.

Source 5

Leaving a gang

Gang life might seem glamorous – but life in prison is far from pleasant, and you're putting yourself, your life, your future, and even the lives of your family members in danger by being part of a gang.

Some tips to help you leave a gang:

- Try to spend less time with the gang and find friends who are not in gangs.
- Try to avoid places where you know the gang will be.
- Speak to someone you trust like a family member, teacher or youth worker.
- You can contact Gangsline for free advice and support from ex-gang members.
- You can call the police by dialling 999 for urgent help if you're in danger.
- Focus on things that you enjoy like sports, music, reading or find new hobbies.
- You can contact Child Line and speak to a counsellor in confidence. They can help you find a way to get out.

Source: www.bedfordshire.police.uk

Source 6

Activity 4

Please listen

Using the information in Sources 1–6 in this topic and your own research, write a speech, letter, blog or article encouraging young people not to join gangs or carry knives.

Your work should be from the perspective of one of the people below and should refer to the reasons people join gangs and carry knives, the impacts they can have on their members and those who are victims and why they should be encouraged to leave.
- an ex-gang member
- a parent of a gang member
- a parent of a gang victim
- the local Police Commissioner.

Activity 5

Funding, gangs and knives

Some people suggest that the amount of funding that is put into things like police numbers and young people's services can have an effect on things like gang violence and knife crimes.

What services or schemes do you think could be introduced to reduce the number of people involved in gangs and knife crime?

8 Identity

8.1 Individual, family and community values

By the end of this lesson you will:
- be able to explain why people have different values
- be able to explain the values that are important to you
- be able to explain what British values are and give your own opinion about them.

Starter

What do you take with you?

When people are faced with a crisis (for example, fire or flood) and have to flee their home, they can only take what they can carry. If you were in this situation, what would you take with you?

Values

In the starter activity you may have decided to take with you objects that have value to you alone and that are irreplaceable because of the meaning they hold for you. The special meaning they have for you will be affected by the values you hold.

Values can be defined as the:
- **qualities**
- **principles**
- **standards**

… of what is important in life.

Source: Oxford English Dictionary

Your personal experiences and your life experiences are different from those of the people around you – everyone is an individual.

Your personal values are:

- your own
- individual
- distinctive
- instinctive
- learned?

Each of us will have individual values, often shaped by our families, our upbringing and where we go to school. There are also overarching 'big' values that often reflect the culture, laws and traditions of a society. These values are shared values. Some are shown in Source 1.

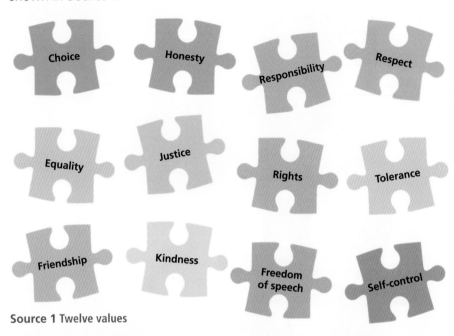

Source 1 Twelve values

Activity 1

Me and my values

How would you answer the following questions for yourself:
- What do I value?
- Why do I value it?
- Where have our values developed from?

Be honest. Remember for the purposes of this activity that your values will not be marked or judged and it is OK to think and act differently from others.

Differences between people are often largely based on a range of different beliefs and values. The importance people put on big values will depend on a variety of factors including their culture, faith and so on. In a multi-cultural society such as ours, people will approach different issues in different ways depending on the values they have. For example, what is our attitude towards care for elderly people? Some cultures and communities value their elders and see caring for them at home as an expression of love and respect for them. Others, while valuing the elderly, do not think that paying others to care for their elderly means they love and respect them less.

Activity 2

Explaining our values

1 We often take the big values listed in Source 1 for granted, and don't make time to talk about what they mean for us. What personal meaning do they hold for you?
   a Decide which:
   - has some importance
   - is important
   - is very important
   - is the most important.
   b Now rank them in order of importance for you.

British values

You may have come across the term 'British values' in your school. These are a set of values that the government has stipulated should be promoted within all schools as they believe they are values that all people in the UK should hold. These values are shown below:

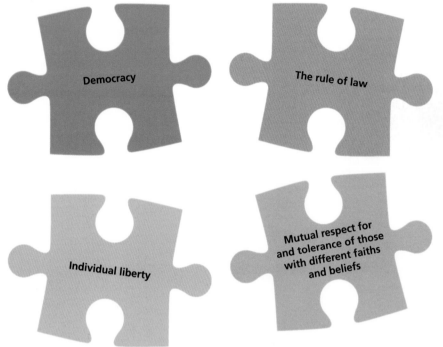

Source 2 British values

By the time you leave school there is an expectation that all students will gain:

- an understanding of how citizens can influence decision-making through the democratic process
- an appreciation that living under the rule of law protects individual citizens and is essential for their wellbeing and safety
- an understanding that there is a separation of power between the executive and the judiciary, and that while some public bodies such as the police and the army can be held to account through parliament, others such as the courts maintain independence
- an understanding that the freedom to choose and hold other faiths and beliefs is protected in law
- an acceptance that other people having different faiths or beliefs to oneself (or having none) should be accepted and tolerated, and should not be the cause of prejudicial or discriminatory behaviour
- an understanding of the importance of identifying and combating discrimination.

Activity 3 looks more closely at 'British values', and Activity 4 explores other situations that will be affected by the values people hold.

Activity 3

Why British values?

1 Do you agree with the values? Explain why you do or don't.
2 Do you think the values are unique to Britain?
3 Why do you think the government felt they had to direct schools to ensure that they promoted British values?

Issue 1: Naseem is worried that the small child next door is not being fed properly. She has not reported this to any authorities yet.

Issue 2: Jack has broken the law and the police have been involved. When asked, his brother Daniel has lied and told the police Jack was at home.

Issue 3: Sophie, a single parent, lives off benefits as she cannot afford to work due to childcare costs.

Issue 4: Dave gets drunk and becomes aggressive towards others when out on a Saturday night.

Issue 5: Mr McKay, a boss of a large financial firm, accepts a huge bonus despite others in the company being made redundant.

Issue 6: Hannah knows that her boyfriend regularly carries a weapon with him.

Source 3 'Issues'

Activity 4

Issues and values

In groups, choose two of the issues from Source 3.

1 Using the values listed in Source 1, decide which could be relevant to each of your two issues. The values you choose may come from different viewpoints. Give examples for each value chosen. For example, tolerance could be one of the values associated with Issue 1 – Naseem might think that she shouldn't interfere as it is not her family.

2 Discuss the values you have decided on for each issue:
   a Which value do you think is the most important in terms of how the community should respond?
   b Which value would most likely help everyone to reach a consensus?

3 Now answer the following questions.
   a Was it easy to see the issue from more than one point of view?
   b How tolerant are we of other people's views when they differ from our own?
   c Were there two or three key values that trumped all the others?

Activity 5

Affirmation

If your school yearbook celebrated you for one of the twelve values listed in Source 1, which would you hope it would be and why?

By the end of this lesson you will:

- understand and practise using different methods of making decisions
- respond to other people's opinions about a range of current issues on which people have different views.
- put forward your own arguments about a range of current issues.

I value my family – my children and my home life. I never bring work home with me and at weekends I devote all my time to family life.

Source 1 What do you value?

Starter

Values and actions

1. We live in a very busy society where some adults seem to have less time to give to family life. What do you think of the values of the parent in Source 1?
2. What value or values do you hold that make you act in a certain way?

In Source 1 the parent made a conscious decision to do something in a particular way; that is, spend more time with their family. Values affect the decisions we make. How often do we stop and think before making a decision?

a Acting on impulse (what I feel like doing there and then).
b Considering the consequences (what might happen).
c Considering the effect it will have on others.
d Doing what everyone else does.
e Doing what my friends say.
f Going along with what's easiest.
g Letting others decide for me.
h Talking it through with someone I trust.
i Trusting my feelings.

Source 2 Ways of making a decision

Activity 1

Deciding how to act

Look at Source 2.

                    1
                 2   3
              4   5   6
                 7   8
                    9

1 How important would each of these approaches
   be in helping you arrive at a decision? Prioritise
   the different ways by putting them into a diamond
   nine as opposite.

2 Now discuss the following questions.
   a Which are the most thoughtful decision-making options?
   b Is it right to go along with others even if you don't support what
      they plan to do?
   c Should you let others make decisions for you?

A The death penalty should be reinstated for those taking the life of
   another person.

B Parents should be able to smack their children if they feel it is
   appropriate to do so.

C Those able to work who claim benefits should have to do
   volunteering work if they are unable to get a job.

D Parents of children who misbehave at school should be made to
   attend parenting classes.

E Students should be able to give grades to their teachers.

Source 3 What's your view?

Activity 2

Different values

1 In pairs, look at the statements in Source 3. Use the nine
   statements in Source 2 as a basis for coming to a conclusion
   about whether or not you agree with each.
2 In pairs, choose one of the statements and write a short speech
   explaining the view you hold and why.

Activity 3

Core values

Is there a particular value that
you would hold to, whatever
the changing circumstances in
your life?

By the end of this lesson you will:

- be able to use appropriate language with understanding when referring to transgender (including non-binary) people
- be able to explain the challenges faced by transgender (including non-binary) people in society
- think of ways in which your own environments could be more welcoming for transgender persons.

Your gender identity is your inner sense and experience of your own gender. For many people, their gender identity will match the gender they were assigned when they were born. Other people might not identify with the gender they were originally assigned and so identify with another gender.

- **Agender:** Someone who does not experience having a gender.

- **Bigender:** Someone who experiences two or more genders either simultaneously or separately.

- **Gender fluid:** Someone whose gender is in flux, and may change over time.

- **Transgender:** Someone who does not identify with the gender they were assigned at birth, often abbreviated as 'trans'.

- **Non-binary:** Someone that does not identify either entirely or exclusively as male or female.

- **Cisgender:** Someone who does identify with the gender they were assigned at birth.

What is important to remember is that someone's gender identity can sometimes be the same as their assigned gender and sometimes it is not – whatever your gender identity is, it is valid and personal.

Terminology

- **Transgender**: This is used to describe people who do not identify with the gender they were assigned at birth. Often abbreviated to **trans**. It is always used as an adjective, for example, 'a transgender woman', 'trans woman', 'transgender man', 'trans man', or 'transgender person' and 'trans people'. It is not used as a noun (e.g. 'a transgender'), nor as a verb (e.g. transgendered).

Source 1 Transgender symbol

- **Non-binary:** A non-binary person has a gender identity that is neither entirely or exclusively male or female. If we were to think of gender as a spectrum, non-binary people may be fluctuating around the spectrum, completely off the spectrum with a gender identity that is neither male nor female at all, or somewhere in the middle. Non-binary people often prefer to use 'they/them' pronouns, but this isn't always the case. If you are not sure it is always ok to ask what pronouns people use.

- **Cisgender:** This is used to describe people who do identify with the gender they were assigned and presumed at birth. Often abbreviated as **cis**. Cisgender is the opposite of transgender. The words cis and trans come from Latin; trans means 'on the other side' and cis means 'on this side'.

- **Transsexual:** A (dated, for many) term used to refer to someone who doesn't identify with the gender they were assigned at birth, and intends to, is currently, or has undergone hormonal and surgical interventions to affirm their identified gender (medical transition). Many may find the term insulting or out of touch due to it being more of a medical term. Only use it when someone has used it about themselves. Some equality legislation uses 'transsexual', but it is defined broadly in such contexts to protect trans people beyond only those who medically transition.

- **Gender dysphoria:** This is the discomfort or distress that many trans people experience over their bodies or how their gender is perceived by others. This discomfort or distress can be related to their primary or secondary sex characteristics, but it is also about how they are treated socially. For example, using the wrong pronouns (for example, he/she/they) for a trans person can cause them significant discomfort or distress. If you would like to know what pronouns a person uses, it is ok to ask them, and maybe even introduce yourself with your own pronouns.

- **Gender expression:** This is how you express your gender identity or how it is perceived by others. Often people assume someone's gender based on how they look; however, it is important to remember that someone's gender identity might not match their gender expression.

- **Transition:** Transition is a social and/or medical process a trans person goes through to affirm their gender identity.

  - **Social transition:** This involves a trans person 'coming out' as transgender. They may (but not always) change their name, the pronouns they use and their gender expression to match their gender identity. This can be a gradual or fast process depending on the person, and they should be free to transition at their own pace.

- **Medical transition:** A medical process of a trans person changing their physiology to better match their gender identity. This may include hormone replacement therapy, surgery or other procedure to alter their primary or secondary sex characteristics. Not all trans people want to medically transition, and some are unable to due to other medical transitions. A person's gender identity is still valid whether or not they medically transition.

- **Pronouns:** Pronouns are words we use to refer to someone without referring to them by name. For example, he/him/his are usually masculine pronouns, and she/her/hers are usually feminine pronouns. There is also they/them/theirs which are gender neutral pronouns. Some trans people use what are known as **neo-pronouns** such as xe/xer/xers (pronounced ze/zir/zirs). These are also gender neutral.

- **Titles:** These are honorifics which are often used before a person's surname, for example Mr Smith or Ms Smith. Mr is usually a masculine title and titles like Miss, Ms, Mrs are feminine titles. There is also the gender neutral title Mx, which is pronounced Mix or Mex. Mx is often used by non-binary people.

Activity 1

What do the statistics tell us?

1   Below are a number of key findings in a 2018 Stonewall report. The percentages have been removed. Have a go at matching up the percentages in the table below to the correct statement and approximate statistics and then discuss the questions that follow.

31%	62%	12%	11%	28%	52%
36%	41%	41%	40%	25%	

- **Two in five** trans people (   ) and **three in ten** non-binary (not identifying as male or female) people (   ) have experienced a hate crime or incident because of their gender identity in the last 12 months.
- **More than a quarter** of trans people (   ) in a relationship in the last year have faced domestic abuse from a partner.
- **One in four** trans people (   ) have experienced homelessness at some point in their lives.
- **One in eight** trans employees (   ) have been physically attacked by colleagues or customers in the last year.
- **More than a third** of trans university students (   ) in higher education have experienced negative comments or behaviour from staff in the last year.

- **Two in five** trans people (   ) adjust the way they dress because they fear discrimination or harassment. This number increases significantly to half of non-binary people (   ).
- **Two in five** trans people (   ) said that healthcare staff lacked understanding of specific trans health needs when accessing general healthcare services in the last year.
- **Three in five** trans people (   ) who have undergone, or are currently undergoing, medical intervention for their transition are unsatisfied with the time it took to get an appointment.
- **More than one in ten** trans people (   ) have gone abroad for medical treatment to alter their physical appearance, including buying hormones over the internet from other countries, with many citing the barriers they currently face in accessing medical treatment in the UK.

2   Do the statistics surprise you?

3   Why do you think some people feel it is acceptable to be prejudiced towards or discriminate against transgender people? (Think back to your work on values.)

4   Do you think the laws that protect all people in the UK, such as the Equality Act 2010, are strong enough in light of the statistics you have just looked at?

Transgender prejudice and discrimination

In the UK, the Government Equalities Office estmate that between approximately 200,000–500,000 people are transgender, although as there is no strong statistical data, this is a best estimate.

However, there is robust data to highlight the fact that those who are transgender are likely to experience prejudice and discrimination in their daily lives.

Charles Thomy

For so long I was embarrassed about who I was. I couldn't tell my parents or friends for fear of upsetting them or driving them away. I turn thirty next week having spent 20 years as a female and nearly 10 as a male. I was a boy when I left school but a female when I left university.

Whilst this was a difficult time in my life, it has turned out to be the most fulfilling with those that I was worried about embarrassing or not wanting to know me, having supported me all the way.

I was hesitant about any medical procedures, as I was worried what people might think, what they might say and whether I was emotionally strong enough to survive this journey. Anyone that I have lost along the way, wasn't a real friend in the first instance. With patience and just being open with others, my family relationships and friendships have grown stronger.

I have changed my name, I have changed my body and as a result my life is happier than it has ever been.

Source 2

Activity 2

Gender concerns

1   Consider Source 2; what concerns and worries did Charles have about changing his gender and why?
2   How could the process of changing gender be made easier?

Activity 3

Values

1   Does the law, or your own personal values, have a greater impact on ensuring that you as an individual treat everyone equally?
2   How could you ensure that your school is a welcoming and safe place for transgender people?

9 Communities

9.1 Living in Britain

By the end of this lesson you will:
- be able to explain different experiences that can unite people from different back grounds positively
- know the benefits of citizen service schemes
- be able to describe the positive perceptions that people have about being British.

Starter

Being human

Imagine the quote in Source 1 with the word *'black'* replaced by any one of a series of words: *disabled, Jewish, old person* and so on. Does the shared experience of being human outweigh all the differences that can separate us?

Maya Angelou was a black, female, American writer – but her thoughts, feelings, joys and sadness are understood and appreciated by all sorts of people across the world. She says: 'I speak to the black experience, but I am always talking about the human condition – about what we can endure, dream, fail at, and still survive.'

Source 1 Being human

Shared experiences unite us far more than our differences divide us. We all want good things for us and those we care about, we all face problems and need to overcome them, we all want to live in a world where we get fair treatment. Although people in Britain come from different backgrounds and cultures, we share much in common.

A survey in 2010, conducted by London Metropolitan University and Sheffield Hallam University, asked people who were training to teach History and Citizenship what they thought of as characteristics of being British. Some of the British characteristics they mentioned are shown in Source 2.

Tolerance   Respect   Fair play   Politeness

Stoicism   Work ethic   Island mentality   Democracy

Queuing   Meritocracy   Snobbery   Rule of law

Being reserved   Christian morality   Xenophobia   Sense of humour

Source 2 What is British?

Source 3 Celebrating new British Citizenship

Activity 1

What is a community?

1 Read Source 2 and discuss/answer the following questions:
  a What is a community?
  b What communities do you belong to?
  c Which seem to be characteristics for building a productive community?
  d Which seem negative?
  e Do you think of these words when you think of 'Britishness'?
  f Would the words change if the survey was done again today?

One characteristic that people often think of as 'British' is a sense of community spirit and people helping each other out in difficult situations.

Source 4 describes the National Citizen Service that was introduced by former Prime Minister David Cameron. One estimated advantage of this scheme was to bring together young people who come from many different communities and backgrounds. The scheme would give them the experience of working together towards shared goals.

The National Citizen Service (NCS)

The National Citizen Service launched in 2011, and due to its success was made permanent through the National Citizens Service Act in 2017.

The scheme takes place during the spring, summer and autumn school holidays and involves groups of teenagers experiencing 'outward bound' style courses including residential ones.

Former Prime Minister David Cameron, who instigated the scheme, said the scheme would encourage people from different social backgrounds to mix, and would help address the 'tragic waste of potential in this country'.

Each young person who takes part spends a minimum of 10 days and nights on activities which will include an outdoor adventure challenge and a set of structured tasks involving visiting and helping the local community. 'The young people of this country are as passionate and idealistic as any generation before – perhaps more passionate,' said David Cameron at the launch.

'But too many teenagers appear lost and feel their lives lack shape and direction. National Citizen Service will help change that. A kind of non-military national service, it's going to mix young people from different backgrounds in a way that doesn't happen right now.

'It's going to teach them what it means to be socially responsible. Above all, it's going to inspire a generation of young people to appreciate what they can achieve and how they can be part of the "Big Society".'

Since its launch in 2011 in which 8000 young people took part, it has grown to almost 100,000 participants as of 2018 and is the country's fastest growing youth programme. Over 400,000 have taken part to date.

Singer Jess Glynne became an ambassador for NCS in 2017, 'It's been really cool and inspiring meeting all the teenagers. When I first got asked to do it, Tinie contacted me and it's been a big eye-opener since then. You don't get taught about livin' at school. You're taught geography, science and maths, not real life things like how to pay bills and the expenses of living on your own. Dreams are also restricted. For me, when I was at school being a musician and an artist was unreachable. It was something I wanted. If someone would've said you can go to music school and pursue your passion I would've loved that. I really think NCS is a great way for young people to learn more about the real world and pursue their passion.'

Source 4

Activity 2

Celebrating citizenship

Source 3 shows a photograph of new British citizens celebrating. In order to become a British Citizen, these people have had to take a test which asks a wide range of questions about Britain ranging from the food eaten to kings and queens.

After taking part in the National Citizen Service (as in Source 4), participants could be recognised as 'active citizens' in a similar celebration to those in Source 3. Draft some key words/ideas for the opening speech that the leader of the ceremony could make. The speech should outline what unites people; what brings them together as citizens.

Activity 3

Being an active citizen

1 Read Source 4 and discuss the following questions. Remember to give reasons to explain your point of view.
   a Do you think the scheme would be popular among your friendship group?
   b What are the advantages of bringing different types of people together through a shared experience?
   c What are the positive things that young people gain?
   d Why do you think a scheme such as this is important for Britain?

By the end of this lesson you will:

- understand what the Equality Act is and its purpose, and be able to list the protected characteristics
- be able to explain what hate crimes are and their impact on individuals and communities
- reach a conclusion as to whether the Equality Act is effective in preventing prejudice
- reflect on whether your own behaviour towards others is always appropriate.

Starter

Equality and discrimination

1 What is equality?
2 What is discrimination?
3 Can you think of any examples from your own experience that illustrate equality and discrimination?

The Equality Act 2010
- Age
- Disability
- Gender reassignment
- Marriage and civil partnership
- Pregnancy and maternity
- Race
- Religion or belief
- Sex
- Sexual orientation

Source 1 The nine areas covered by the Equality Act 2010

The Equality Act was introduced in 2010 with the aim of replacing previous anti-discrimination laws. This law applies to everyone in Britain and protects them from discrimination. It covers nine main areas, shown in Source 1.

The Act protects you from discrimination in the following ways:

- when you are in the workplace

- when you use public services like healthcare (for example, visiting your doctor or local hospital) or education (for example, at your school or college)

- when you use businesses and other organisations that provide services and goods (like shops, restaurants and cinemas)

- when you use transport

- when you join a club or association (for example, your local tennis club)

- when you have contact with public bodies like your local council or government departments.

In summary, the Equality Act means that everyone must be treated equally in all walks of life. If it can be proven that someone is being treated differently because of one of their protected characteristics, for example, being gay, then legal proceedings can begin against the person or company discriminating, supported by the law.

Case study 1

When two men were refused a double room at a family-run bed and breakfast, they decided to take legal action against the owner. The host offered the couple (who were not civil partners) a twin-bedded room but refused to give them a double bed on religious grounds, stating their belief that sex before marriage was a sin and 'against God's law'.

Case study 2

A man who supported the campaign to legalise same-sex marriage in Northern Ireland commissioned a cake to take to a private party being held to celebrate International Day Against Homophobia. The baker agreed to supply the cake but refused to decorate it with the requested message.

Case study 3

A woman was left angry and upset after being asked to stop breastfeeding her baby on a Ryanair flight. She was flying back from Portugal and had read that having a baby breastfeeding would help prevent their ears popping during take-off and landing. She had done this on a previous flight and so didn't think it would be a problem. However, a steward came over and told her to stop breastfeeding her child, waiting until she had unlatched her child and re-dressed.

Case study 4

A mother with a seven-year-old daughter who cried every day because she had to wear a skirt to school feels that the school should change their strict uniform policy which only allows girls to wear skirts. The mother argues that discrimination against girls at the school is occuring as boys and teachers can wear trousers, and has threatened the school with legal proceedings. However, Philips High School in Bury have started a petition against a trousers-only policy, with girls at the school stating 'We feel more confident wearing a skirt and school trousers are unflattering'.

Hate crimes

A hate crime is a criminal offence that is perceived by the victim, or any other person to have been motivated due to prejudice towards someone based on their personal characteristics, identified in the Equality Act.

Hate crimes can include: threatening behaviour, assault, robbery, damage to property, inciting others to commit hate crimes and harassment. At present, almost 80 per cent of hate crimes involve race.

A victim of a hate crime does not actually have to be a member of a particular group, for example, they may be targeted as they are wrongly assumed to be gay. Such an incident would be recorded statistically as a hate crime.

Activity 1

The Equality Act

1 What is the Equality Act? Give a brief summary.
2 Read through case studies 1–4, and for each decide whether or not you think the Equality Act has been broken. Discuss your thoughts with a partner before discussing as a class.

Since hate crime figures were first published by the Home Office in 2011, the number of hate crimes recorded has continued to increase. This is due to improvements made in how hate crimes are recorded, but it is also thought to reflect actual rises in the number of these crimes. Source 1 shows particular 'spikes' in race hate crimes, following three well-publicised events.

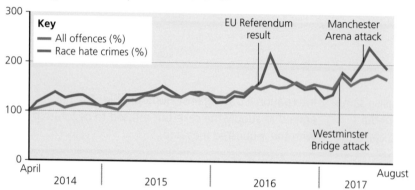

Source 2 Race hate crimes recorded by police in England and Wales.
Source: the Office of National Statistics

Activity 2

Media and hate crimes

1   Do you think the media reporting of such events contributes to the increase in hate crimes?
2   At present the figures released don't include hate crimes that may be linked to age or gender. The government has announced a review to decide if these should be included. What do you think?

What do the statistics tell us?

94,000 hate crimes were recorded by the police in England and Wales in 2017/18. That's an increase of seventeen per cent on the previous year and more than double the number five years ago.

Hate crimes represent about two per cent of crimes recorded by the police.

The majority of hate crimes recorded by the police are based on race (76 per cent).

There was a 'clear spike in hate crime' around the time of the EU referendum, according to the Home Office: both during the campaign and after the result was announced.

One in eight hate crime offences result in a suspect being charged or a witness being summonsed to appear in court. Nearly three quarters of cases halt because of difficulties in finding evidence, identifying the suspect, or getting the victim's support for further action.

About 14,000 hate crime prosecutions took place in 2016/17. That's down two per cent compared to the previous year.

Hate crimes convictions are leading to harsher sentences. When people are convicted of hate crimes the CPS can apply for what's called an 'uplift' – this means they are asking for the sentence to be increased. In 2017/18, two thirds of hate crimes successfully prosecuted by the CPS involved an uplift.

In 2016–17:

- 62,685 (78 per cent) were race hate crimes
- 9 157 (eleven per cent) were sexual orientation hate crimes
- 5 949 (seven per cent) were religious hate crimes
- 5 558 (seven per cent) were disability hate crimes
- 1 248 (two per cent) were transgender hate crimes.

Source: www.fullfact.org

Source 3

Police issued an appeal after a gay couple, who had just enjoyed a Valentine's Day dinner, were subjected to a homophobic attack on a train by a group of men.

One of the men reported that he had tried to get away and that the men had followed him and continued to assault him. He was unable to defend himself.

After being punched and kicked, the two men were admitted to hospital with their injuries. Both were left with bruising and cuts and one lost two teeth, while the other suffered a suspected broken eye socket.

The police issued CCTV images of the attackers and the British Transport Police (BTP) confirmed that one of the five men had come forward to speak to them. The other four men were still wanted in connection with the attack.

Source 4

Research has shown that people often don't recognise their behaviour towards others as criminal activity, particularly some forms of online and verbal abuse. A joint campaign by the Crown Prosecution Service and other organisations was launched to educate the public about what a hate crime is.

The strapline of the campaign sends a clear message:

> 'If you target anyone with verbal, online or physical abuse because of their religion, race, sexual orientation, disability or transgender identity – you may be committing a hate crime. It's not just offensive. It's an offence.'

The campaign which launched on 31 October 2018, included adverts running on video-on-demand sites, social media and posters displayed across the country.

Each video or poster featured a different offender, represented by an e-fit, and a hate crime taking place.

These include:

- a lesbian couple being verbally abused at a bar
- racist graffiti being sprayed on the shop of a foreign couple
- an offender posting hate-filled messages about a transgender woman online
- a Muslim woman being aggressively shouted at to remove her headscarf and a Jewish man being abused in the street
- a disabled man being verbally abused on a bus.

Activity 3

Impact of hate crime

Read through Sources 2–4 and then discuss the following questions with a partner, before sharing your ideas as a class.

1. What are the impacts on those involved in the cases described in Sources 2–4? Consider:
   a. their individual emotions at the time of and after the attack
   b. the impact on the wider community.
2. Other than the improvements to the reporting process of hate crimes, why else do you think more hate crimes are being reported?
3. Do you agree with the idea of 'uplifting'? Why do you think it was introduced?
4. Why do you think it is sometimes difficult to find evidence to support criminal proceedings with regards to hate crimes?

Activity 4

Reducing ignorance

1. How effective do you think the government campaign is to make people aware of what hate crimes are?
2. Were you aware of the fact that such behaviours were actually criminal offences?

103

By the end of this lesson you will:

- be able to explain what is meant by the prejudice of invisibility
- investigate how and where LGBTQ+ and other minority groups are portrayed on TV
- know how prejudicial language can cause harm.

Invisibility

Starter

Who can you name?

1 Can you name five national or international figures who are:
   - disabled?
   - from black, Asian and minority ethnic groups?
   - lesbian, gay, bisexual or transgender?
2 Which list was hardest to compile – what does this tell you?

The previous topic looked at examples of discrimination and how they could be challenged. It is easier to challenge prejudices when we are aware of them. However, one form of prejudice not so easily tackled is that of 'invisibility'. In other words, not including any representation of people who may be different.

Even though things have improved, it may be that people of some ethnicities, religions, cultures, abilities or disabilities, genders, ages or sexual orientations are featured less in news reports, TV programmes, films, novels, adverts and so on, and as a result, become 'invisible' in the media.

While the number of LGBTQ+ (that is those who identify themselves as lesbian, gay, bisexual, transgender or queer/questioning, etc.) have increased in terms of their exposure on TV and through the media, there is concern that these are generally 'gay white men' and other LGBTQ+ characters are still lacking.

The prejudice of invisibility is explored by using some examples associated with lesbian, gay, bisexual, transgender and queer/questioning people.

Activity 1

Unseen on TV

Read Source 1 and discuss and answer the following questions:

1 Do the comments in the article surprise you? Why?
2 Looking back over the last few months, can you identify a positive and negative example of LGBTQ+ people/characters on TV?
3 LGBTQ+ people are not the only group that can end up being invisible. Do a short comparison survey looking at these examples: people with a physical disability and/or a learning disability;

people who are overweight; senior citizens; people with mental health problems.

a In which programmes have you seen them and how were they portrayed?
b What perception does this lead you to have and how could it make people feel?
c Consider your own school. Are these identities visible in your school? If not, how could it be improved?

Unseen on screen

Groundbreaking research published by Stonewall has found that ordinary gay people are almost invisible on the 20 TV programmes most watched by Britain's young people.

Young people from across Britain interviewed by researchers said that gay people on TV are largely stereotyped as leading unhappy lives and bullied and rejected by their families. They also said they rely on TV to learn about gay people.

Researchers monitored 20 TV programmes most popular with young people on BBC1, BBC2, ITV1, Channel 4 and Channel 5 for a 16-week period. This revealed that ordinary lesbian, gay, bisexual and transgender people are practically invisible.

Just 46 minutes out of 126 hours of output showed gay people positively and realistically. Almost half of all portrayal was stereotypical, with gay people being depicted as figures of fun, predatory, promiscuous or tragic.

- 39 per cent of portrayal was in soap operas and 33 per cent was in reality TV.
- There was negligible reflection of gay people in magazine shows and talent shows and no portrayal in drama programmes.
- There were 39 minutes that made passing reference to gay people – half of these references depicted gay people largely for comic effect.
- Almost 20 per cent of references used being gay, or the possibility of being gay, to tease or insult.
- 17 minutes of programming depicted homophobia but 59 per cent of this went unchallenged. Just seven minutes featured scenes where homophobia was challenged.
- 17- and 18-year-old young gay people simply don't relate to gay people they see on TV.
- Young people want to see positive and realistic portrayal of LGBTQ+ people on TV and think it would have a positive effect on their own attitudes and behaviour and that of their peers.

Source 1

Activity 2

What Do We Do with a Variation?

1 Read Source 2. What do you think is the message of this poem?
2 Consider your own experiences at school and the resources you use in lessons, such as novels in English and textbooks in other lessons. Are minority groups represented equally and fairly?

What Do We Do with a Variation?

by James Berry

What do we do with a
difference?
Do we stand and discuss its
oddity
or do we ignore it?

Do we shut our eyes to it
or poke it with a stick?
Do we clobber it to death?

Do we move around it in rage
and enlist the rage of others?
Do we will it to go away?

Do we look at it in awe
or purely in wonderment?
Do we work for it to
disappear?

Do we pass it stealthily
or change route away from it?
Do we will it to become like
ourselves?

What do we do with a
difference?
Do we communicate to it,
let application acknowledge it
for barriers to fall down?

Source 2 A poem by James Berry

By the end of this lesson you will:

- understand that different forms of prejudice exist and explain some of the impacts
- think about whether your own actions towards people with protected characteristics are appropriate
- devise your own ideas to combat prejudice and discrimination.

Starter

What can people do?

'Rosa sat so Martin could walk so Barack could run.'

Who are these people and what do you think this quotation means?

Syrian and Afghan refugees arrive by boat from the western coast of Turkey at Limantziki beach, Eftalou, Greece (2015)

This unit is about diversity and appreciating the similarities and differences between human beings. Sometimes people discriminate (intentionally and unintentionally) against things or people that they find strange, or do not understand. This lesson addresses three different types of discrimination and uses examples for each:

- **prejudice** – attitudes towards refugees and asylum seekers
- **ignorance** – not knowing enough about and being afraid of HIV
- **thoughtlessness** – overlooking or not considering the needs of people with disabilities.

In each case you will be encouraged to think about taking the initiative in challenging these and other forms of discrimination.

Prejudice

The first source and activity looks at **refugees** and **asylum seekers**. It provides a window through which to look at some of the difficult decisions they have to make through necessity rather than choice.

Colnbrook immigration removal centre near Heathrow airport is a short-term holding facility used to hold people immediately after their detention by the UK Immigration Service

Refugees and asylum seekers

A refugee is someone who flees from their own country for safety. This may be as a result of war, natural disaster or being persecuted for reasons such as their race, religion, nationality, political opinion or membership of a particular social group.

An asylum seeker is a person who applies for protection and the right of residence in a foreign country.

The number of people forcibly displaced by conflict and persecution worldwide stood at 68.5 million in 2018. The total includes 25.4 million refugees and asylum seekers and 40 million internally displaced people uprooted within their own countries.

About 85 per cent of the world's refugees live in developing countries, often in camps. Africa, Asia and the Middle East between them host more than three quarters of the world's refugees. Europe looks after about 15 per cent. The UK is home to less than two per cent of the world's refugees.

The reporting of conflicts in countries such as Syria and the refugee and asylum crisis that has followed has raised concerns that the reporting of the media in the UK has increased levels of prejudice. A study in 2016 by Cardiff University's Journalism School found that British press reporting was 'aggressive' when compared to other European countries. While some newspapers featured humanitarian stories to encourage sympathy, many reinforced a hardline anti-refugee and migrant approach.

Source: Eurostat

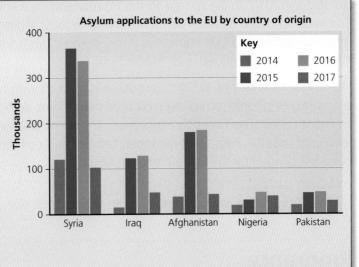

Asylum applications to the EU by country of origin

Source 1

Activity 1

Having to leave

Read Source 1. Refugees and asylum seekers generally receive very little empathy and understanding over their situation. This activity is about exploring how people feel when they are forced to make difficult decisions to become a stranger in a new country – and not by choice.

1. When you get home there is a note on the kitchen table saying you must leave in half an hour. You do not know where you are going or how long for, or if you will ever see your home again. You can only take a small rucksack. List the 10 items that you want to take with you.

2. Also on the kitchen table are three tickets. These have been incredibly difficult to obtain because they are rationed. Decide which two people out of all your family and friends will come with you.

Over here and out of control

Migrants stealing British jobs

Army called to stop migrants invading

Migrants threaten to kill British truckers

Source 2

Headlines such as those in Source 2 have been linked to a rise in support for political parties that are considered to be prejudiced. This is not just in the UK but in other European countries too. Parties and groups like this are often referred to as 'far right'. An article in *The Conversation* in 2017 used statistical analysis to show how increased media coverage of a particular issue such as migration led to increased support for certain political parties that have what some view as anti-immigration policies.

Activity 2

Discussion

Read Source 2.

What did Jo Cox mean by the statement *'We have more in common ... than that which divides us'*?

On 16 June 2016, in the run-up to the EU referendum, Labour MP Jo Cox was murdered by an extreme rightwing terrorist. Thomas Mair shot and stabbed Jo Cox numerous times saying, 'This is for Britain, keep Britain independent' and 'Britain First'.

The first anniversary of Jo Cox's murder was marked with hundreds of thousands of people picnicking with their neighbours across the UK in an event called 'The Great Get Together'. The event was to spark the feeling of togetherness at a time when families and communities had been left divided by the EU referendum result.

> 'We have more in common … than that which divides us'
> Jo Cox

Ignorance

Source 3 and Activity 3 move on to look at discrimination caused by ignorance. People often fear something because they don't truly understand it, and then they make judgements before knowing the true facts.

50% of HIV sufferers face discrimination

The Terrence Higgins Trust found that half of people living with HIV have experienced discrimination because of their status. A recent poll to coincide with the charity's Zero HIV campaign found:

- two thirds said fear of HIV discrimination has impacted on their mental health
- according to the charity, half (50 per cent) of people living with HIV have experienced discrimination because of their HIV status.

Effective treatment shrinks the amount of virus in the body to undetectable levels, which protects the immune system from damage and means HIV can't be passed on to anyone else. Despite this progress, and the fact that people diagnosed with HIV today can thrive, misinformation around HIV still causes stigma, which impacts many people living with HIV.

People said about living with HIV:

- it had made an impact on their mental health (60 per cent)
- it made them feel unable to talk openly at work, with friends, family or when dating
- it made them feel alone (50 per cent).

Ian Green, Chief Executive of Terrence Higgins Trust said: 'As ending HIV transmissions in the UK becomes a reality, we must support those living with the virus to thrive, and end the stigma they face. We must not just focus our efforts on reaching zero transmissions, but also zero stigma.'

Source: Terrence Higgins Trust

Source 3

Activity 3

HIV discrimination

Read Source 3 and discuss the following questions:
1 Do you understand how HIV is transmitted?
2 Look at your school's equal opportunities policy to find out if discrimination against people with HIV is covered.
3 Are there other school policies that ensure people with HIV won't suffer from discrimination?

Thoughtlessness

The final source and activity look at how people with disabilities are viewed, treated and often represented by others. It uses a media example of this prejudicial and thoughtless discrimination.

Prejudicial attitudes

In 2009 the BBC employed presenter Cerrie Burnell to work on their children's channel, CBeebies. Cerrie was born with only one hand and when she appeared on television the press revealed that complaints were sparked from parents who claimed that the CBeebies host was frightening their children.

There were reports that some parents said they would prefer it if their children did not see or hear about people with disabilities.

A father explained that he didn't want his children watching because he felt it would have played on his daughter's mind and possibly caused her sleep problems.

Other parents felt that it was forcing them to discuss disability before their children were ready. However, there were also those who expressed their support for the presenter and the BBC, voicing that if a child asks questions then they are old enough to understand the answer. Some parents felt children simply accept the world as presented to them and did not have problems in accepting people with disabilities. A few revealed they were delighted to have been given the opportunity to talk about people's differences and everyone being individual. One person verbalised the rich diversity of the world we live in, explaining that if parents are so negative about encountering people who are different from them (whether it be religion, skin colour, height, weight, disability, etc.) their child will be growing up with a distorted view of reality.

A handful went on to applaud the BBC for employing someone for their ability to do the job, irrespective of any disability.

Speaking for herself, Cerrie said, 'That this has happened at all is really just a sign that we need to have more disabled people on telly.'

Source 4

Activity 4

Point of view

Read Source 4.
1 What do you think of the different attitudes expressed in it?
2 Despite progress in the last few years in terms of diversity on TV, most of the people we see are still, for example, able-bodied, attractive, slender and under 45 years old. How do you feel about that?
3 Write a letter to the BBC explaining your point of view and expressing your opinions as a future television licence payer.

Activity 5

Combating prejudice

In pairs, come up with a list of ideas that could help combat prejudice on an individual/local scale such as your school community.

Activity 6

Discussion

'It is harder to crack a prejudice than an atom.'
Albert Einstein

What is it about prejudice that makes it so difficult to combat?

While laws such as the Equality Act have helped reduce prejudice and discrimination to some extent, both still exist. While people may not be openly prejudiced, they may still harbour thoughts about particular groups in society. This is often borne through ignorance, for example, a lack of understanding and knowledge about a particular group.

Growing evidence suggests that we are more likely to make friends with people who are similar to ourselves, but mixing with a diverse set of people can stimulate creativity, which benefits both individuals and society. So how do we achieve this?

By the end of this lesson you will:
- be able to explain how different types of government operate and how voting processes work
- know what is needed to be eligible to vote and why it is important to do so
- decide if you agree with the current UK voting system.

Starter

Democracy

1 What is democracy?
2 In Wales they are considering lowering the voting age to 16. Do you think other UK countries should do the same? What are the advantages and disadvantages of such a decision?

The United Kingdom is a democratic society (democracy). This means that we get to have a say in how the country is run. We may agree with the way things are, or want a change, so when we are asked to do so we can vote to let our view be known.

The most common opportunity to vote is at a local council or general election. These happen every four to five years and the public get to vote for the political party they wish to see running the local area, or running the country.

There are also other opportunities to vote. At a local level, if you are a member of a sports club, you may be asked to vote for the club president; in school, you may be asked to vote for a school council or student voice member. At a national level, you may be asked to vote on other significant issues affecting the country as a whole. For example, in 2014, people in Scotland were asked to vote on whether or not they wanted Scotland to be independent of the UK. In 2016 a vote in a referendum was held to decide if the UK should remain part of the EU, the result of which you will no doubt be aware of.

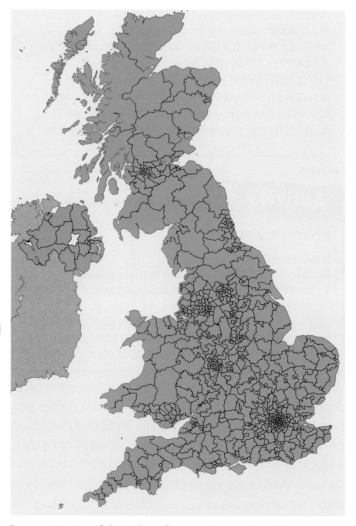

Source 1 A map of the UK's parliamentary constituencies

The Electoral Commission state that to be eligible to vote in UK elections, you must be registered to vote and:

- be 18 years of age or over on polling day
- be a British, Irish or qualifying Commonwealth citizen
- be resident at an address in the UK (or a UK citizen living abroad who has been registered to vote in the UK in the last 15 years)
- not be legally excluded from voting.

First past the post

In the UK we run a 'first past the post' system to decide who our government becomes. This means that the person (candidate) who gets the most votes becomes the Member of Parliament (MP) for their local area, known as a constituency. Their job is to represent the views of the people that voted for them in Parliament. The political party that gets the most MPs then becomes the new government. In total, there are 650 constituencies represented by 650 elected MPs.

Three well-known political parties in the UK are: Conservatives, Labour and Liberal Democrats. In recent years though, other political parties have also become more prevalent in terms of the media coverage they have received. These include The Green Party, UK Independence Party (UKIP), Democratic Unionist Party (DUP), Scottish National Party (SNP) and Plaid Cyrmu. There are also many other smaller political parties.

In the run up to an election a political party will produce a manifesto, which is basically a list of the things they stand for. If they become the new government, they will try and implement the things they have stated in their manifesto. For example, in the run up to the 2017 elections, the Green Party stated the terms of their manifesto, shown in Source 1.

The 2017 Green Party manifesto pledged to:
- campaign for the people's right to vote on the final terms of the Brexit deal, including an option to stay in the EU
- lobby for affordable, warm homes for everyone and a free public health system for all
- fight for equality, and for a society where nobody gets left behind
- act strongly on climate change and to protect the natural world
- stand up for what matters.

Source 1

Activity 1

First past the post

Use the internet to research the advantages and disadvantages of the first past the post system of voting and any other alternatives to this.

Activity 2

Your manifesto

1 In groups, write a manifesto for your own political party. Give your party a name and make a list of the things that you would stand for, and try to achieve if elected.
2 Present your ideas to the rest of the class.
3 Were there any similarities between the different groups? If so, why do you think this was the case?

Voting

One of the key roles of an MP is to vote when new laws are being made. For a new law to be approved at least 326 MPs must vote in favour of it.

In 2018, the Conservative Party won the general election, with 318 MPs being elected. This meant that they couldn't pass new laws without MPs from other political parties supporting them and therefore did a deal with the DUP to support them in return for more money being invested in Northern Ireland.

Despite the importance of voting in elections, some people choose not to. In 2017, 69 per cent of the people in the UK that were eligible to vote actually did, meaning that nearly a third chose not to.

In some countries around the world, people do not get the right to vote, or the elections are set up so that there is only one political party to vote for, giving no real choice to the people. These countries are often referred to as dictatorships.

Source 2 Nazi Germany

When Hitler became leader of Germany in 1933, one of the first steps he took was to outlaw other political parties, meaning that his party's decisions could not be questioned. Those that did try to challenge the authority of the Nazi Party could be threatened, beaten, imprisoned or even killed.

Another example you may be familiar with is that of North Korea. While its official title, the Democratic People's Republic of Korea, suggests it is a democracy, the reality is very different. Elections are held, but only one name appears on the voting (ballot) paper. Everyone is expected to vote and consequences of not doing so could lead to you being investigated. The Kim dynasty has ruled North Korea since 1948.

Source 2 North Korea

The Democracy index

In 2018, a report by *The Economist* ranked the best democracies through to the worst. Countries were ranked on a scale of 0–10 based on civil liberties, the electoral process, government functionality, political participation and political culture.

Activity 3

Research

1 In pairs, use the internet to research a country that appears towards the bottom of the democracy index. Find out what the day-to-day lives are like for the people in the country. Compare their lives with the lives of people in the UK.
2 Produce a Venn diagram that shows the differences and similarities between your chosen country and the UK.
3 Should the 'best' democratic countries try and impose their political beliefs and way of life on those that appear towards the bottom of the list?

Democracy index

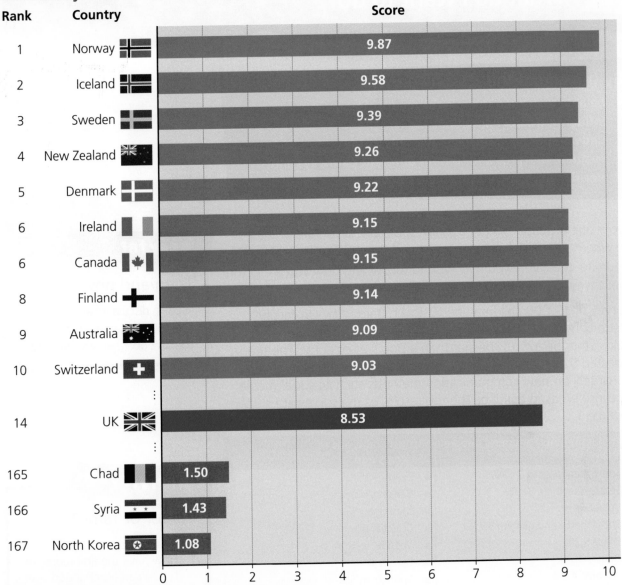

Rank	Country	Score
1	Norway	9.87
2	Iceland	9.58
3	Sweden	9.39
4	New Zealand	9.26
5	Denmark	9.22
6	Ireland	9.15
6	Canada	9.15
8	Finland	9.14
9	Australia	9.09
10	Switzerland	9.03
14	UK	8.53
165	Chad	1.50
166	Syria	1.43
167	North Korea	1.08

Source 3 The best and worst countries for democracy, 2018

Activity 4

Compulsory voting

Australia is one of 23 countries in the world where voting at general elections is compulsory. Failure to do so results in a small fine of around £12. Some regard this as contradictory to what a democracy is. Considering one in three did not vote in the 2017 UK general election, do you think a law should be passed making it compulsory for all eligible voters to actually vote?

10 Planning for the future

10.1 What do I want to do?

By the end of this lesson you will:

- be able to explain the role the media can play in influencing career ambitions
- understand the 'pathways' available at the end of KS4
- evaluate the 'pros and cons' of different pathways and decide which you may be most suited to.

As your age increases, so does your responsibility. You are at the age now where you will be thinking more and more about the next stage in your life, the career you may wish to follow and how you are going to get there.

A survey of 13,000 children aged 7 to 11, backed by University College London in 2018, showed that primary school children would rather be a YouTube star than a pop star or actor. The report suggested that there has been a 'shift in the aspirations of children' built largely on new communication methods such as social media and console-based gaming. The top results of the survey are shown in Source 1.

Top ten ambitions for young people in 2018	Top ten ambitions of 25+ years ago
■ Sportsman/woman 21.3%	■ Teacher 15%
■ Teacher/Lecturer 10.9%	■ Banking/Finance 9%
■ Vet 6.9%	■ Medicine 7%
■ Social media and gaming 5.7%	■ Scientist 6%
■ Police 5.2%	■ Vet 6%
■ Doctor 5.2%	■ Lawyer 6%
■ Scientist 4.2%	■ Sportsman 5%
■ Artist 3.9%	■ Astronaut 4%
■ Singer/Musician 3.8%	■ Beautician/Hairdresser 4%
■ Army/Navy/Airforce/Firefighter 3.3%	■ Archaeologist 3%

Source 1

As long ago as February 1968, the artist Andy Warhol said *'In the future everybody will be world famous for fifteen minutes.'* Since that time there has been the birth and growth of reality television and growing fame among YouTube and vlogging stars. This has made fame seem more possible for the general population.

In addition the cult of celebrity has grown, and now reporting on celebrities has become prolific. Young people are encouraged to believe that anyone can become a celebrity – they can become famous for being famous, not necessarily based on talent and ability.

Starter

Then and now

In pairs, discuss what you are able to do legally now, that you couldn't do when you were 12.

Activity 1

Career or fame?

Look at Source 1.
1 How have the ambitions for future careers changed over 25 years?
2 Why do you think they have changed?

114

Reality check: life behind Insta-glam image of 'influencers'

Online they feature in glossy posts as the epitome of cool. But that is often worlds apart from how they live their lives.

Standing amid the reeds and staring pensively into the distance, Jordan Bunker looks every part the moody model, dressed head to toe in black – in a direct contrast with the setting. Another image from his portfolio shows him in industrial environs, sporting a minimalist brown trench coat as he looks directly at the camera.

However, the reality for the 24-year-old is far from the glamour associated with the fashion world. In his pyjamas in bed – he's fighting a cold – at the home he shares with his parents in Leicester, Bunker says his set-up is worlds apart from the pensive street-style glossy shots of him kitted out in designers Paul Smith, Grenson and Joseph on his Instagram page, which has amassed 17,500 followers.

'All isn't how it is perceived on Instagram,' he says. 'People assume I have a great life and everything is handed to me. I live with my parents and I work from a desk in my room; it's not like I have a separate working space or office.'

Bunker is one of a growing army of 'micro-influencers', social media personalities with a following of between 10,000 and 100,000.

The growth of social media has resulted in the rise of the influencer who, at the top end, can make millions a year through the endorsement of products.

But these high earners are a very small minority: those like Bunker earn significantly less, while still maintaining the attention of thousands of young people.

While regularly seen dressed in on-trend menswear, Bunker is actually on a modest freelance income of about £30,000, with most stemming from social media, blog posts and guest talks.

'It's quite a humble salary but I'm quite proud of it,' he admits. He charges between £500 and £1,000 to promote a brand on his Instagram feed or blog.

The scale of the industry is substantial and growing – market research firm Statista says the value of the global Instagram influencer market is set to reach $2.38bn in 2019 from $1.07bn in 2017.

Earlier this year, more than a dozen celebrities, including Alexa Chung and Ellie Goulding, pledged to change the way they label social media posts after the competition watchdog clamped down on the practice of stars being paid for endorsing products without disclosing they were being rewarded by the company.

Source: *The Guardian*, 17 March 2019

Source 2

Case study

Mike MacCraigie

Mike MacCraigie is a bright student at a City Academy in the Midlands. Tests predict he should do well in his GCSEs but he struggles to concentrate. Instead, Mike has his eye on becoming a footballer, ideally for his beloved Birmingham City FC.

'Footballers get loads of money and I enjoy playing it as well,' he says. 'Everyone knows who you are when you are a footballer, you are worldwide. I would just love the lifestyle.'

Mike recognises it is tough to make it in football, especially as he does not have a clear idea how to turn professional. He has also been told to have a back-up plan in case his dream does not come true, so he is spending one day a week at Birmingham Metropolitan College, learning about bricklaying and other trades.

The 15-year-old admits he does not always value qualifications. He says: 'You do not need them to become a footballer. All you need is skill.'

Source 3

Activity 2

Real or fake?

Read the article in Source 2. Work in small groups to discuss the article and whether you think young people are too readily influenced by social media vloggers in terms of their employment aspirations.

Activity 3

Read Source 3.

Mike is thinking of leaving school without taking his GCSEs. What arguments would you use to convince him to think again?

Aspirations about your career are likely to change throughout your life, and many factors will influence the decisions you make, including the law. While you might not be seen as an adult in the eyes of the law until the age of 18, you are legally allowed to do certain things at different stages on the way to adulthood. This can also mean you are legally responsible for your actions. Remember, you have a responsibility to know what you can legally do at your age so it's important to know what's what.

One of the most important decisions you will need to make in the near future is what you will choose to do at the end of Year 11. The decision you make at this point will start you on your career path, so it is important to know what options are available to you.

There are three main pathways you could follow, as shown in Source 4.

Finish compulsory education or training

Pathway 1:
Full-time learning in a school sixth form, sixth form college, FE (further education) college, with a training provider or UTC (university technical college).

Pathway 2:
Employment such as an apprenticeship, job with training or a traineeship.

Pathway 3:
Spend 20 hours or more a week working or volunteering, while in part-time education or training.

University
You may decide to go to university to study; this will give you even more options when you come to seek employment.

Having gained further qualifications, you could now follow Pathway 2 or 3.
The qualifications you have gained will mean that you have more options when seeking employment and your earnings may be higher.

Source 4 Pathways

Activity 4

What are my options?

1 Using the information in Source 4, draw your own flow diagram that shows the pathway you might follow. Include as much detail as you can; for example, you could include the name of a college, specific subjects you would like to study or types of voluntary work. Your teachers will be able to provide further information, as will careers advisors and school and college websites.

2 You may find that some sections of your flow diagram are more difficult than others to complete as you don't yet have the information you need. Make a list of all the questions you need answers to in order to add further detail to your flow diagram, for example: What courses are available at my local college? How would I be expected to travel there? If I went into an apprenticeship, how much would I earn?

3 In groups, discuss your questions with each other to see if anyone has similar questions, or if anyone is able to help you answer the questions you have.

4 As a class, make a list of the questions that still remain unanswered. Discuss who or which organisations would be able to provide the information needed.

5 From your list of questions, select three that are of interest to you. Make a note of these and over the next week see if you can find the answers to them. Feed back in your next lesson what you have found.

Risks

Any pathway you choose comes with risks, both financially and in terms of your overall career progression. The trick is to weigh up the advantages and disadvantages of each pathway while considering the type of person you are. For example, if you are someone who enjoys school, a sixth-form course may be more suitable; if you haven't really enjoyed your school life but do want to have additional training, you may choose work-related training. Remember it is what best suits you!

Activity 5

What are the risks?

Make a copy of the table below. Using the information in Source 5, fill in the table to show the advantages and disadvantages of each pathway option (some of the advantages and disadvantages could relate to more than one option). Add any others you can think of.

	Full-time education	Work-related training, e.g. traineeship	Part-time education – 20 hours work/ volunteering
Advantages			
Disadvantages			

Pathways - pros and cons

a   could lead to a large debt
b   earn straight away
c   higher qualifications to put on CV
d   increased competition as more students apply
e   keep options open
f   leads to a skilled trade/profession
g   less chance for promotion
h   likely to lead to a higher paid job

i   low/no income
j   lower earnings
k   lower pay until qualified
l   more employment options open to you
m   most friends follow a different pathway
n   nationally recognised qualifications
o   valuable experiences; for example, travelling.

Source 5

Activity 6

Where will you be?

Working in pairs, talk to your partner about the flow chart you completed in Activity 5. For each stage of your chart, think of the challenges you may face. Offer advice to each other about how these challenges could be overcome. Do you face the same challenges?

By the end of this lesson you will:
- understand advantages and disadvantages of different types of employment
- be able to explain how financial aspirations and other factors can influence career options.

Job, occupation, career, vocation, employment and work are all terms commonly used to describe what is expected of us when our formal education is over. Although these terms do have slightly different meanings, they all basically refer to the fact that the majority of people will enter 'the world of work' when their formal education is at its end.

The world of work will be different for everyone and, to begin with, this is dependent largely on what has been achieved during formal education. The types of work people do can be split into three main categories:

■ **Employed**

A person who is employed is known as an employee. They will work for an individual or company and receive a wage or salary. The majority of people in work are employees.

■ **Self-employed**

A person who is self-employed will work for themselves and keep track of their own earnings. It is likely that they will be highly skilled, perhaps in a trade such as plumbing, or they will have a niche product to offer.

■ **Voluntary work**

A voluntary worker is a person who doesn't get paid for the services they offer. They are often associated with charity and support work, but could actually be involved in a wide range of work.

Each type of employment has advantages and disadvantages that need to be considered before entering into the world of work. Some of these are shown in Source 1 on the next page.

Starter

Types of employment

1 Under the headings 'Employed', 'Self-employed' and 'Voluntary', put the jobs shown in Source 1 on the next page into the correct category (some could fall in more than one – explain why, when this is the case). Add to your lists so that for each category you have eight different jobs.

2 Look through your lists and highlight the jobs in each list that you would most like to do if you had to choose.

3 Now work with a partner and explain to them the reasons why you highlighted your particular jobs. Were your partner's reasons for choosing their jobs the same as yours?

Activity 1

Pros and cons

Make a copy of the table below. With a partner, brainstorm the advantages and disadvantages of each category.

	Employed	Self-employed	Voluntary
Advantages			
Disadvantages			

a) Solicitor
b) Accountant
c) Lifeguard
d) Farmer
e) Firefighter
f) Television producer
g) Working in a soup kitchen
h) Dressmaker
i) Removal person
j) Software engineer
k) Plumber
l) Environmental worker

Source 1 Different jobs

Career paths

There are many factors that influence someone's work or career choice. These include interests and resulting job satisfaction, whether you have the appropriate skills and qualities to match the job, and the amount of money you can earn and potential future earnings.

For most people entering the world of work for the first time, there is a long and hard pathway in front of them before they can earn the amount of money they would like. You have to 'work your way up' in terms of your training, experience, references and eventually earnings. This is known as the career path, and it begins in school. The better the results you achieve in school and the longer you stay in education or training, including sixth form and university, the more opportunities you are likely to have to follow a career path that leads to a higher paid job. However, staying in education for longer, such as going to university, has a cost. The Institute of Fiscal Studies has stated that in 2017 the average debt for students leaving university was £50 000. It is important to remember though, that loan repayments are calculated based on what you earn and not what you borrowed. You also need to be earning a certain amount before you start to pay it back.

Once you have your education 'under your belt' it is important to be able to use the skills and knowledge you have developed to gain employment so you can develop your skills further and earn a living.

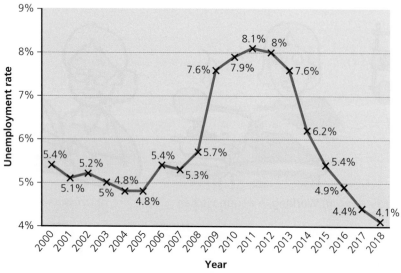

Source 2 Unemployment in the UK 2000–2018

Source 2 shows unemployment rates from 2000 to 2018. As you can see, the number of people unemployed generally declined, until 2008 when the country went into recession. However, recent figures have shown that unemployment is at an all time low. These aren't all high paying jobs. Many are low paid jobs including employees on 'zero hours' contracts. Using graphs such as this we are able to work out **employment trends**. If we looked at statistics dating back even further we would notice that unemployment rates rise and fall many times.

So what is likely to happen in the future? History shows us that employment rates rise and fall, influenced by many different factors, but what are the key trends at the moment and how might they change in the future? Source 3 supplies some information about this.

Activity 2

Employment trends

Select three of the boxes about employment trends in Source 3 and for each one think of a reason/reasons why this trend is likely to happen.

Activity 3

Your future

Using the information you have learned in this topic, write a paragraph explaining how your own future could be affected. You need to consider the following factors:
- the type of employment you may enter into
- how your education could influence this
- the cost of your education and who pays
- unemployment rates
- future employment trends.

---

a More fluidity in the job market – meaning people will regularly move from one job to another, 'job hopping' – particularly for highly skilled workers.

b Self-employment will continue to increase as numbers of highly paid jobs available decreases.

c It is estimated that around two-thirds of the new jobs will go to women and that around two-thirds of all the new jobs will be part-time.

d Most workers will have between 20 and 25 jobs in their working lives.

e A higher importance will be placed on workplace perks, for example, flexible working hours, staff discounts and so on.

f Greater focus on diversity within employees.

Source 3 Employment trends

By the end of this lesson you will:

- compile your own CV
- practise other effective ways to present personal information
- create your own personal branding and profile.

For someone to make the world their oyster they need to be able to develop their skills and qualities in order to achieve as much as they possibly can.

Qualifications, qualities and skills for employment

In order to practise veterinary medicine in the UK, most vets will be members of the Royal College of Veterinary Surgeons (RCVS). They will need a degree from a university recognised by the RCVS or to have passed the MRCVS examination.

We can see that everyone needs more than just qualifications and skills to make the most of their lives. Each of us has qualities that we use socially and in the world of work. In addition to assessing your skills and abilities, you also need to be able to recognise and reflect on your personal qualities. This will help you when thinking about your future career plans.

Personal qualities

a   Careful – you take care of your own and others' feelings.

b   Courageous – you stand up for what you believe in and don't shrink away from challenges.

c   Creative and original – you are an innovative thinker and full of new ideas.

d   Critical thinker – you think things through before taking action.

e   Curious and interested – you like exploration and discovering new things.

f   Enthusiastic and energetic – you approach projects with excitement and energy.

g   Fair and principled – you do not let your personal feelings bias your decisions.

h   Good team player – you always do your share and work hard for the group.

i   Hard worker – you don't get distracted and you meet your deadlines.

j   Honest and genuine – you are down-to-earth and try to be yourself.

k   Kind and generous – you enjoy doing things for other people and are willing to offer time and help.

l   Leader – you are a good organiser and will encourage everyone in the group to get things done.

Source 1

Starter

The world is your oyster

What do you think the saying 'the world is your oyster' means?

Activity 1

What's the difference?

1   What's the difference between a qualification, a skill and a quality?

2   A vet will have to have particular qualifications (see above). But what qualities would it be good for a vet to have?

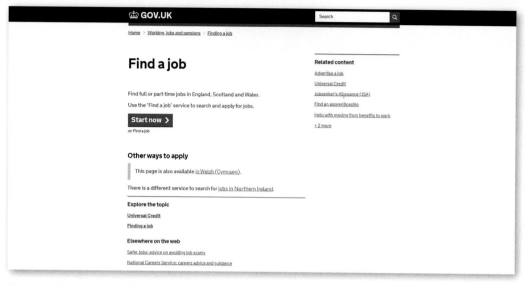

Source 2 Website for self-assessment

Writing a CV

When applying for a job (even a part-time one) your prospective employer will probably want to get a sense of what kind of person you are. Being proactive in this process impresses potential employers and you may want to consider:

■ phoning up to arrange a meeting so that you can introduce yourself

■ setting up your own blog and drawing attention to it

■ attending 'networking events'

■ creating a professional online profile using websites such as LinkedIn.

In most cases when applying for a job you will be asked to send in your **Curriculum Vitæ (CV)** or complete an application form, which as well as including contact details, qualifications and work experience, should also include some of the personal hobbies and interests you have. This is important as it gives the employer some indication of what you are like.

Activity 2

Personal qualities

Look at Source 1 and score yourself against the list: A score of 5 means that you are strong in the quality. A score of 1 means you do not have much of this quality in you.

Activity 3

Further ways to self-assess

1 The websites featured in Source 1 are a starting point when thinking about future careers. Explore these to help you identify the types of skills and qualifications you will need to develop for the career path you would like to follow.
Here are websites:
https://www.gov.uk/find-a-job
https://www.prospects.ac.uk/careers-advice/cvs-and-cover-letters/create-a-great-video-cv

2 What are the qualities you need to develop in order to help you achieve what you want to in the future?

Good ... better ... best!

Jane is preparing a list of her personal hobbies and interests for a job application. Here are three ways she could describe her interests.

- Reading, cinema, keeping a scrapbook, crafting.

These interests could imply she is a solitary individual. Although there's nothing wrong with preferring your own company, an employer will most likely be looking for evidence of teamwork or contributing to something.

- Reading, cinema, keeping in touch with my 'exchange' friend, socialising.

This sounds a little better.

- Cinema: member of the school film club.
- Travel: a summer exchange trip – visited historic sites and practised my French and Spanish with the family and friendship group there.
- Reading: helped younger pupils with reading difficulties at school.

Jane is still the same individual as in the first example, but here the impression is much more detailed and shows she is a proactive individual who helps others.

Source 3

What is a CV?

A CV is an outline of a person's education and work experience. (It means, literally, 'the course of one's life'.) It is usually prepared for job applications. Another name for a CV is a résumé.

A CV is the most flexible and convenient way to make applications. It should convey your personal details in a way that presents you in the best possible light. It is useful to leave a copy with the people you're hoping to get a job with; for example, when you're asking around for a weekend/holiday job.

Sometimes employers ask for an application form instead. This is designed to bring out the essential information and personal qualities that the employer requires. Preparing a CV (even though you can't submit it) can save you time when filling out these forms as all the information about you is already set out in one place.

There is no one best way to construct a CV – it is your document and can be structured as you wish within a basic framework. You could send it in on paper or complete it online if that is what the employer asks for. If you're applying for something particularly creative you may find another way to present your CV, for example, a Facebook profile or a blog page!

Source 4 shows an example of a 16-year-old student's CV with comments that highlight and explain its different aspects.

Activity 4

The best of me

1 Look at Source 3. Why do you think an employer might be more favourable to the third example?
2 What's the best way to describe your interests? First brainstorm a list of words to identify your interests, then work in pairs to write a bullet list that outlines your hobbies and activities in an interesting and useful way – remember you want to make a prospective employer interview you.

Activity 5

My CV

1 Compile your own CV. Look at Source 4 and try and follow the good advice for setting out your skills and experience. Use the interests you identified in Activity 4 in your CV.
2 Work with someone else and look at each other's CV. Identify areas for improvement in light of the advice given in Source 4 and make suggestions to help the other person.

Include your name, address, date of birth (although with age discrimination laws now in force this isn't essential), telephone number and email.

Nick Alexander: Curriculum Vitæ

4 Somewhere Close, Weald Gate, HA24 7PE
Phone: 020 0031 7245 (home) 06752 932 100 (mobile)
Email: nick@nicksworld.com
Nationality: British
Age: 16

Keep this section short and to the point. Bullets can be used to separate the text.

Anything showing evidence of employability skills. Here Nick has shown he can work with others.

Achievements and interests

- Attended Weald Gate High School for the past five years and have every intention of entering the sixth form in September 2019.
- I currently help younger pupils, in Year 7, with reading support.
- Captain of school tennis team.
- Whilst a student in Year 9 I attended an international camp in Spain where I continued my National Curriculum education alongside pupils from South America, Russia and European countries. The experience was invaluable in terms of gaining responsibility, independence and the confidence to communicate and interact even when there was a language barrier.
- My hobbies include skiing, tennis, working out at the gym, cinema and theatre.

Don't include many passive, solitary hobbies – show a range of interests to avoid coming across as narrow. If everything centres around only one type of activity they may wonder if your focus is too narrow or you need more life experiences.

Any evidence of leadership is important to mention, e.g. captain or coach of a sports team.

Include extra curricular activities and life experiences that are relevant for future work.

Work experience/Employment

2018 – Kutz Hair and Beauty Salon, High Road, Weald Gate, Hampdenshire
As a 'junior' I undertook duties that ranged from cleaning the salon, making coffee for staff and clients, washing hair and working on reception to cover absences and breaks.

2018 – The Elms Tennis and Football Club, Weald Close, Weald Gate, Hampdenshire
I helped organise and lead a team who supported children aged 5-13 years in playing games, and learning to play tennis. My responsibilities also included pastoral welfare at break and lunchtimes.

Nick uses action words such as 'organise' and 'lead'.

Try to relate the skills to the job. Nick has prepared this CV for a position working with young people.

Work in a shop, bar or restaurant will involve working in a team, providing a quality service to customers and dealing tactfully with complaints.

Education and qualifications

2014-2019 Weald Gate High School

GCSE subjects:

Art; English; ICT; French; Maths; Physical Education; Religious Studies; Science

Your subjects can also highlight your skills, such as languages and computing.

References

Frank Byers
Owner/MD
Kutz Hair and Beauty Salon
High Road
Weald Gate
Hampdenshire
Tel: 020 0031 7322

Virginia Lawn
Managing Director
The Elms Tennis and Football Club
Weald Close
Weald Gate
Hampdenshire
Tel: 020 0031 8787

Usually two references are sufficient. These could be from school and from an employer (perhaps your last part-time or summer job).

Source 4 An example of a CV

Personal branding

While a good CV is still considered one of the best ways to 'sell' yourself to prospective employers, the internet and social media have opened up a variety of other means to develop your own 'personal branding'.

Recruitment website **Jobvite.com** states that for the purposes of actively recruiting and advertising to new employees, 93 per cent of companies use LinkedIn, 66 per cent use Facebook, and 54 per cent use Twitter, with 73 per cent of recruiters having actually hired candidates through these social media channels.

Video CVs to complement a written CV are becoming increasingly common. They can help your own CV stand out against the competition and despite the perception they are only applicable to certain jobs, for example, customer facing and creative roles in sales and marketing, they can make a difference in any sector of employment. The following points should be considered when making a video CV:

How to create a video CV

- Dress to impress – just as you would for an interview.
- Write a plan, and memorise what you can – it's fine to have notes as a cue, like a newsreader, but don't read them straight from your notepad.
- Introduce yourself – including your contact details at the end.
- Think about the background in shot – ensure it's free from posters or other distractions.
- Record the video in a quiet environment.
- Showcase your work portfolio – through a slideshow, clips or a screenshot of your website.
- Tell a story – make sure it has a beginning, middle and end.
- Come up with three unique selling points (USPs) you want to get across to employers.
- Watch it back, and edit out anything that doesn't put you across in the best possible way.
- Utilise free online tools and hosting.

Source: www.prospects.ac.uk

Source 5

With such easy access to people's lives through social media, 93 per cent of potential employers now review a candidate's social media profile before making the hiring decision. Depending on what they see could have an impact on their final decision. It is therefore important that you consider what you post online, as your digital footprint is likely to be there forever. No doubt you will know of stories in the news in which people have been forced to resign because of things they posted online, even if it was many years ago.

Activity 6

Your online profile

1 What is your own online profile and personal branding like? What impression would potential employers have of you if they saw your social media accounts? What would you change?
2 Think of three strap-lines to describe yourself to employers. For example:
   - Ambitious
   - Confident
   - Successful

By the end of this lesson you will:

- be able to explain the benefits of good relationships between employers and employees
- understand what trade unions are and give examples of how they support workers
- be able to explain the rights and responsibilities you will have when employed.

Regardless of the work you do, there are certain rights and responsibilities that all employers and employees have. Within the UK, clear employment laws are in place that set out specific rights that have associated responsibilities for both employers and employees (see Source 1).

A responsible employer will:

- give their employees a contract of employment that sets out terms and conditions such as pay, hours, holidays, the type of job you will do and the leave period you need to give or can expect to receive when your employment ends
- enrol you in a pension scheme
- provide employees with an itemised payslip
- pay employees at least the national minimum wage
- give all workers the same pay for doing the same job, as per the Equality Act 2010
- give part-time and full-time workers the same rights
- give employees reasonable time off for specific events such as family emergencies
- give employees paid holiday
- give women time off during pregnancy for antenatal care and up to 52 weeks' maternity leave
- give time off with pay for paternity, adoption and shared parental leave
- give parents unpaid time off as appropriate to be with their young children, particularly if the children are under five or have disabilities
- follow health and safety guidelines as laid out by law
- give statutory sick pay to those who are entitled
- give redundancy pay to workers who have been at a company for at least two years and are laid off
- treat all workers the same as per the Equality Act 2010.

The employer has a great deal of responsibility to ensure that all the rights of the employee are met. However, employment is a two-way thing and the employee also has responsibilities.

Source 1

Starter

Responsibilities

1   Make a list of all the different responsibilities you think an employee should have, for example, being punctual and starting work on time.

2   Go through your list. Highlight those which are also appropriate to you at school.

Discuss the following questions:

3   Are you always as responsible as you should be in school? If not, why not? If yes, why do you think it is important to be responsible?

4   What happens when someone behaves irresponsibly at school? What is likely to happen if someone behaves irresponsibly at work? Are there any differences?

Although employees are protected by employment laws, many employees also choose to join a trade union, which offers them further 'protection' at work.

There are occasions when union members may vote to strike if they feel that compromises with their employer aren't being reached. Source 3 shows some details of a strike that took place in 2018.

The main aims of trade unions are to:

- negotiate agreements with employers on pay and conditions
- discuss major changes to the workplace, such as large-scale redundancy
- discuss their members' concerns with employers
- accompany their members in disciplinary and grievance meetings
- provide their members with legal and financial advice
- provide education facilities and certain consumer benefits, such as discounted insurance.

Source: www.direct.gov.uk

Source 2

Ryanair Pilots' Strike 2018

When Ryanair pilots walked out on strike over pay and conditions, flights were cancelled for tens of thousands of passengers across Europe. The pilots' union wanted the Ryanair employees' contracts to be governed by the laws of the country they are based in, and not on Irish laws, which is where Ryanair orginates from. Despite the Civil Aviation Authority stating that Ryanair was responsible for giving passengers their money back, the airline refused to pay compensation, leading to thousands of complaints.

Source 3

Activity 1

Unions and strike action

1 Why are trade unions important for employees when we already have employment laws that are in place to protect workers?
2 Read Source 3. What would be the impact of strike action by Ryanair pilots?
3 Most of the teachers in your school will be part of a union. What would be the impact (both short and long term) if they voted to strike over pay and conditions?
4 Can you think of any jobs in which workers might not be allowed to strike? Why would they not be allowed?
5 The organisation National Union of Students (NUS) is a union set up for students. Imagine that you are setting up a student union in your school. Produce a leaflet/poster/manifesto outlining what you stand for, what services you would provide and the rights and responsibilities students, staff and the school have. The NUS website may help you with some ideas – www.nus.org.uk.

Activity 2

Just a minute

In pairs, play a game of 'Just a minute'. You must talk for one minute about rights and responsibilities at work without pausing or hesitating. Your partner needs to listen carefully to see if you repeat yourself. Once you have had a go swap with your partner.

By the end of this lesson you will:

- investigate the types of jobs that are available to you in different locations
- research employment opportunities using the internet
- evaluate the pros and cons of working abroad.

The world of work has changed rapidly over the last 15 years and is continuing to do so. One of the main reasons for this is the development of high-speed internet and mobile communications, which means that ideas and information can be shared instantly at the touch of a button.

Another way in which things have changed is where people choose to work. As a result of improvements in communication, transport and trade relations, businesses have been able to set up all over the world and employees have been given the same opportunities.

When looking for work it is important not only to know what is available, but also where. To fulfil your career aspirations you may find that you need to move in order to get the job you desire.

Amazon is now one of the world's biggest companies. Founded in 1994 by Jeff Bezoz, it is now worth over $1 trillion.

Source 1 Amazon recruitment poster

Starter

What can a big company offer?

Look at Source 1. Make a list of all the employment opportunities a company such as Amazon could offer.

Activity 1

Categories of work

1. Use the internet to look at a number of jobs online. You could use websites such as www.reed.co.uk. How many jobs can you find for each of the categories in Source 2?
2. Discuss the following questions.
   - Which category of job was the most and which was the least common?
   - What does this activity tell you about the local labour market?
   - Which jobs are most likely to be there in the future? Why?
   - Which jobs are most likely to disappear in the future? Why?
   - Are there any jobs that you have found that are of interest to you? If yes, explain why you are interested in them; if no, explain what type of job you are interested in and why.
   - Where else could you get information about local jobs?

Different categories of jobs

- Administration, business and office work
- Building and construction
- Catering and hospitality
- Computers and IT
- Design, art and crafts
- Healthcare
- Education and training
- Engineering
- Environment, animals and plants
- Financial services
- Personal and other services including hair and beauty
- Languages, information and culture
- Legal and political services
- Leisure and sport
- Manufacturing
- Retail, sales and customer services
- Marketing and advertising
- Media, print and publishing
- Performing arts
- Science, mathematics and statistics
- Security and armed forces
- Social work and counselling services
- Transport and logistics

Source: Adapted from www.jobs.ac.uk

Source 2

If you are unable to find a job that interests you locally, you may need to consider looking further afield.

Activity 2

Looking for work

1 Go to **https://www.gov.uk/jobsearch**. Click on 'start now' and the 'browse all jobs' at the bottom of the page. You will be presented with a list of categories of jobs from all over the country. Glance through the list and click on any that take your interest.

2 Choose ten different jobs, and for each one mark their location on a map of the UK. You may need to use an atlas to help you find the different locations. Next to each location write down what the job is, the salary and any other key information.

3 In small groups, discuss the locations you have found for your particular job. Would you be prepared to move? Are you likely to find the same job locally? How would you feel if you had to move away from family and friends?

Working in Europe

Britain has long held a close political, social and economic relationship with Europe. As a result of this, there has often been plenty of opportunity to live and travel in Europe.

Some UK citizens may decide to seek out jobs in Europe.

The map in Source 3 shows the number of UK nationals of working age (15–65) in other EU countries in 2011.

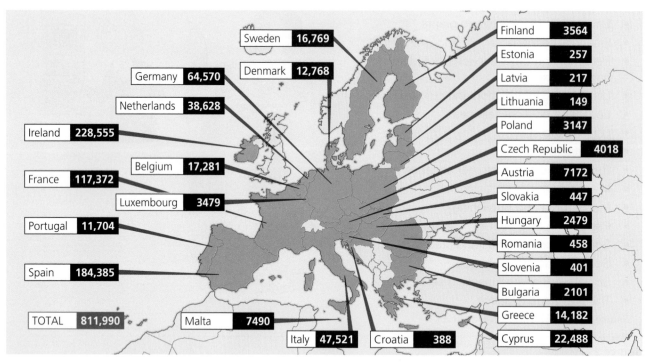

Sweden	16,769
Denmark	12,768
Germany	64,570
Netherlands	38,628
Ireland	228,555
Belgium	17,281
France	117,372
Luxembourg	3479
Portugal	11,704
Spain	184,385
TOTAL	811,990
Malta	7490
Italy	47,521
Croatia	388
Finland	3564
Estonia	257
Latvia	217
Lithuania	149
Poland	3147
Czech Republic	4018
Austria	7172
Slovakia	447
Hungary	2479
Romania	458
Slovenia	401
Bulgaria	2101
Greece	14,182
Cyprus	22,488

Source 3 Number of UK nationals working in EU countries, (based on the last National Census in 2011)

Activity 3

Working in Europe

1 Source 3 shows that the number of British people working in Europe was not evenly distributed. Suggest reasons why more British people might have chosen to work in Germany, Ireland, Spain, France and the Netherlands in particular.

2 Using the internet, go to **www.eurojobs.com**. Think back to the jobs you looked at in Activity 2 and use the website to search for similar jobs. Are the details similar?

3 What incentives would you need to pack up, leave Britain and work in a European country? Discuss your reasons in pairs.

Migration

Being close to Europe also means that people from other countries can seek employment in the UK. You may have read or heard headlines such as these examples:

Eastern Europeans taking our jobs

How many more can we take?

Cheap labour costs us jobs

Migrant workers out of control

Source 4 Headlines about immigration

Headlines such as these never truly give the full story about economic migration – it is a highly complex issue which is dependant upon many factors.

Working beyond Europe

If you are unable to find the job or lifestyle you want within Britain or other European countries, you may decide to look further afield. With transport and communication being as good as they are today, people now have the whole world in which to seek employment opportunities.

The process of being able to work in countries outside of Europe is more complex. You are likely to need documents such as visas and work permits, have a minimum amount of money in your bank account, have medical checks and also be immunised against certain illnesses before you are allowed to move.

Activity 4

Migration, media and prejudice

1 Why do you think that newspapers and other media sources write such provocative headlines as those on the left?
2 What is the likely impact on the individuals and communities being referred to in such headlines?

Activity 5

Working across the world

1 Make a list of all the positive and negative factors of moving outside of Europe to work.
2 Despite the complex processes, the potential rewards for working beyond Europe can be huge, not only financially but also in terms of satisfaction.

It is now estimated that 5.5 million British people live and work permanently throughout the world – almost one in ten of the UK population. The top five countries can be seen in the table below – what do they all have in common?

Country name	Resident Britons
Australia	1,300,000
United States	800,000
Canada	700,000
New Zealand	315,000
South Africa	305,000

Activity 6

What about you?

1 Can you ever see yourself moving away from your local area to work? If so, how far do you think you are likely to go – national, European or global?
2 Do you think your attitude will change with time? Explain your answer.

By the end of this lesson you will:
- be able to explain why we pay tax and what it is used for
- practise budgeting for a new home
- practise planning for a secure financial future.

Why do we need to pay tax?

1 What would happen to society if we didn't pay tax? Discuss all the problems we would face, for example, those who couldn't afford to pay for their own healthcare would have to go without treatment.

2 Look at Source 2. Do you think it is fair that different people pay different tax rates depending on how much they earn? Explain your answer.

Most people would like to have more money; the amount of money you earn has a direct impact on your lifestyle. Having 'lots of money' means that you can do the things you really want to do or buy the things you really want to buy. Having 'just enough' money could mean that you only just get by and have to be careful what you spend your money on. You are more likely to spend it on things you need as opposed to things you want.

Most people earn money by working. The money you get paid for working is your wages and you receive a pay slip to show how much you have earned. When you get your pay slip you will see two different section – payments, which summarises the income you receive; and deductions, which summarises money being taken off your total pay to cover your tax and national insurance payments. This is shown in Source 1.

Two different payments

Employee No.	Employee Name			Process Date	National Insurance Number
12	Mr. Dave Smith			15/05/2019	KT893548S

Payments	Units	Rate	Amounts	Deductions	Amount
Salary	1.00	3386.10	3386.10	PAYE Tax	479.72
				National Insurance	322.09

Mr. Dave Smith
25 High Street
Lincolnshire

LN12 8PL

This Period	
Total Gross Pay	3386.10
Gross for Tax	3386.10
Earnings for NI	2482.45
Payment Period	Monthly

Year To Date	
Total Gross Pay TD	6772.20
Gross for Tax TD	6772.20
Tax Paid TD	1159.23
Earnings for NI TD	5414.23
National Insurance TD	658.32

Superfast and Local Ltd

Tax Code: 458P   Dept 5   Payment Method: BACS   Tax Period: 1

Net Pay	2584.29

Source 1 A pay slip

Tax and National Insurance rates

In 2019/20 everyone could earn up to £12 500 before they have to start paying tax. Once you earn more you pay tax at the rates shown in Source 2.

In addition to paying tax, you will also be expected to pay National Insurance contributions if you earn more than £8632 per year. National Insurance contributions are taken to pay for a number of things including: the NHS, unemployment benefit, sickness and disability allowances and state pension.

Amount earned	% of earning paid in tax
£0–£12,500	0
£12,500 to £37,500	20 (basic tax rate)
£37,500 to £150,000	40 (higher tax rate)
Over £150,000	45 (additional rate)

Source 2 Percentage of tax paid

You can also be charged tax on the following: earnings from self-employment, most pensions' income, interest on most savings, income from shares (dividends), rental income, income paid to you from a trust.

Category letter	£118 to £166 a week (£512 to £719 a month)	£166.01 to £962 a week (£719.01 to £4167 a month)	Over £962 a week (£4167 a month)
A	0%	12%	2%
B	0%	5.85%	2%
C	N/A	N/A	N/A
H	0%	12%	2%
J	0%	2%	2%
M	0%	12%	2%
Z	0%	2%	2%

Source 3 National Insurance rates 2019/20

Most employees have a category letter A. Your category can be found on your payslip.

Category letter	Employee group
A	All employees apart from those in groups B, C, J, H, M and Z in this table
B	Married women and widows entitled to pay reduced National Insurance
C	Employees over the State Pension age
J	Employees who can defer National Insurance because they're already paying it in another job
H	Apprentice under 25
M	Employees under 21
Z	Employees under 21 who can defer National Insurance because they're already paying it in another job

Source 4 Employee categories. Source: https://www.gov.uk/national-insurance-rates-letters

Mortgages

Unless you have an endless supply of money you will need to budget your income carefully, particularly if you want to buy your own home in the future.

Most people buy their own home with the help of a mortgage. A mortgage is a legal agreement in which a loan is provided for a customer to purchase a property. Usually a customer will need a cash deposit (approximately five per cent of the property price, although this can vary) and the rest of the money will be provided by the bank or building society they have made the agreement with. The customer then repays the mortgage according to the terms in the agreement.

Source 5 Mortgage application

The two main ways to repay a mortgage are 'repayment' and 'interest only'. With a repayment mortgage you make monthly repayments for an agreed period (usually 25 years, although due to the rising cost of living, many younger people are taking on 40-year mortgages) until you've paid back the loan and the interest. The interest rate will vary depending on the type of mortgage you choose.

With an interest-only mortgage you make monthly repayments for an agreed period but these will only cover the interest on your loan (endowment mortgages work in this way). You'll normally also have to pay into another savings or investment plan that will (hopefully) pay off the loan at the end of the term.

Depending on the type of repayments you are making you could end up paying back twice the amount you borrowed. Although this sounds very expensive, it does allow people to own their own property and have a secure investment, providing they have kept up with their repayments.

Activity 1

How well could I budget?

Megan is 19 years old. She has just finished college with qualifications in hospitality, and has been offered a job at a local hotel which has the potential to lead to a management role. Her starting salary is £19,458 per year, which after tax and National Insurance would leave her with approximately £1400 per month. She lives with her mum and step-dad at present, but is keen to move into her own place. She has found a one-bedroom flat around the corner from where she currently lives, which is advertised for £525 per month.

1   Make a list of the different things Megan would have to pay for on a monthly basis if she moved into a one-bedroom flat, for example, mortgage or rent, water rates, Council Tax and so on. Include essentials such as food, but also other things that Megan might like to have in her home.

2   Try and put a monthly monetary value on each of the things on your list. Your teacher will be able to give you some ideas about costs or you could research them on the internet. When you have the monetary values, add them together to get a total.

3   Go back through your list and highlight things that are essential in one colour and things that are desirable in another. For example, if you have included satellite TV you need to think whether this is really necessary.

4   Work out your new monthly expenditure based solely on the essential things.

5   Based on your costings, would you recommend that Megan moves into the flat, or stays living with her mum and step-dad until her salary increases further?

Savings

Remember that in addition to the essentials you need to spend your money on, you will also want to have money left to buy other things that you want.

The money you have left after paying for all your essentials is known as your **disposable income**. This is the money you may choose to buy new clothes, pay for movie subscriptions or games with, or go out for dinner, the cinema or whatever else you like to do. Another option, however, is to consider saving or investing some of your disposable income for the future.

You could save into your regular (current) bank account. This will mean that you can access the money as and when you need it by using you bank/debit card. However, if you intend to save some money on a regular basis there are other types of savings accounts that will earn you more interest. One example of this is through a type of account called an Individual Savings Account, often know as an ISA. ISAs are tax-free savings accounts, which means you do not have to pay tax on any interest earned.

To get the best deal on bank and savings accounts it is important to shop around to see which offer you the best deals. Some will offer other incentives such as free overdrafts or mobile banking.

Source 6 What could you afford if you saved money on a regular basis?

Activity 2

Which account should I choose?

1 Research and select one bank account you think would be most suitable for you to have your wages paid into each month, and one savings account that would be best to save into. Some of the comparison websites such as **www.moneysupermarket.com** are particularly useful for researching this as they give you a quick overview of each account. You will need to find out the following things about each type of account:

Once you have selected the most appropriate account for you, write down the details.

2 In small groups, explain to each other why you have chosen your particular current and savings account:
   - What were the advantages and disadvantages of each account?
   - What was the most and the least important factor when deciding?

Current account	Savings account
Which bank it is with	Which bank it is with
Cost of banking (often free)	Minimum monthly payments needed
Overdraft facility	Interest rates
Type of card provided	How quickly you can access funds
Interest given on money in account	Other incentives
Overdraft facility & cost	
Amount needed to open account	
Other incentives	

Pensions

Another way to save for your future is a pension. This is a source of income that people receive when they retire. You may have heard a great deal of talk about pensions recently.

This is because the population as a whole is ageing and therefore more people need greater support financially, for longer. You may find that you will be expected to work to at least 70+ to receive your state pension, rather than retire at the current age of around 65. The pension age for men and women has already risen to 66 from the year 2020.

When planning your retirement there are three main types of pension you need to consider. These are:

- the state pension
- personal pensions
- company pensions.

State pension

The state pension is a regular payment people can claim when they get to state pension age. Most people build up some state pension, but the amount they get varies depending on how many years they have paid National Insurance contributions – to get the full state pension you need to have contributed for 35 years.

Personal pensions

Personal pensions (also known as private pensions) provide you with a regular income in your retirement. It works by making regular payments during your working life, and the more you can afford to pay in, the more you will receive when you retire.

Company pensions

Company pensions are set up by employers to provide pensions for their employees on retirement. They are also sometimes called occupational or workplace pensions. Both the employer and employee contribute to this type of pension scheme.

Activity 3

The dream retirement

1 Describe the type of lifestyle you would like to have when you retire.
2 Consider all the things you will need to do as from now to achieve this, and make a plan. In your plan show the different stages of your life and what you will need to do at each stage to achieve your retirement lifestyle. You could include the stages 16, 18, 24, 40, 50, 60 and 70+. You will need to include details about education, career choices, mortgages, savings and lifestyles.

Activity 4

Planning for my own future

How important do you think it is to plan for your financial future?

By the end of this lesson you will:

- understand how advertising encourages the spending of money
- be able to decide if 'offers' are really as good as they suggest
- know ways by which you can reduce your own waste.

Special offers?

1 Look at the information in Source 1. What special offers are described? Can you think of any others?
2 Have you or a family member ever:
   - bought an item of clothing from a sale and then not worn it
   - thrown away food from a two-for-one offer because it went off before it could be used
   - ended up realising it wasn't such a 'good deal' after all the extras were added?
3 Do you think you have ever been taken in by any of these?

All sorts of things affect our choices as consumers (for example, cost, taste and appearance, brand loyalty, ethical concerns such as food miles, fair trade, animal testing, impact on environment and so on). In this topic you are going to look at what it means to be a responsible consumer, and in particular you are going to look at how the following might influence our choices:

- price/special offers as a factor in influencing choice
- concerns around how supermarkets deal with waste.

One way of defining a responsible consumer is:

> Somebody who understands but is not taken in by the power of persuasive advertising. They are able to be socially responsible and selective over what they purchase.

Special offers? *Money Matters* and *Which?*

The responsible consumer can spot the real bargain ...

Shops are full of special offers, but some of them aren't that special, and even break government guidelines.

Organisations such as 'Which?' investigated offers at high street and online retailers to check if they complied with government guidelines to ensure that offers don't mislead customers. They found:

- Some pricing tactics encourage spending unnecessarily, with complex pricing including '2 for 1' and 'Buy One Get One Free' (BOGOF) offers. Three in ten consumers said that BOGOF offers resulted in them throwing away unused food.

- Some retailers, including airlines and gig and concert promoters, use 'drip pricing', where the cost of an item grows through the buying process; extra charges, for example, taxes, credit card fees or delivery, are revealed only when a buyer is part way through the process.

- Some retailers use 'baiting' techniques, for example, clothing shops using banner headlines saying 'Half Price Sale', when only some items are available at discounted prices.

Source 1

Responsible consumerism

We would all like to think of ourselves as responsible consumers but inevitably most of us get drawn into buying things. One way to look at our own spending habits is to think of our 'Wants versus Needs'.

1   Make a list of everything you can remember buying (or that was bought for you) in the last six months. Categorise them into 'wants' or 'needs'.

2   Work with another person to compare your lists. Did you find they had the same views on what constituted needs?

3   How easy is it to be socially responsible and selective in the face of sophisticated and persuasive advertising?

Source 2 £13 billion of food is thrown away by households in the UK every year, having a damaging effect on the environment.

Food wastage

The Waste & Resources Action Programme (WRAP) found that there was significant food wastage across the UK, for example:

■   10 million tonnes of food and drink waste was thrown away from our homes and businesses in 2016.

■   Of this, 4.2 million tonnes was avoidable, worth about £13 billion.

■   Nineteen per cent (by weight) of food and drink brought into the home is thrown away. Food waste that is disposed to landfill generates methane, a greenhouse gas far more powerful than carbon dioxide. Not wasting good food and drink would have the same positive environmental impact as taking one in four cars off UK roads.

■   Food waste in the home is not the only source of food waste, but WRAP's work shows it makes the single largest contribution – around 50 per cent of total food waste in the country.

Why do people buy more food than they can use? Supermarkets need to provide more information so that responsible consumers can make informed choices. Consumers need to let supermarkets know what change is needed.

In 2017 it was announced that the East of England Co-op would become the first major retailer to sell food beyond its 'best before' dates.

The chain is independent of the Co-operative group and has 125 stores in East Anglia. In an attempt to reduce food waste, it was decided that each store would sell dried foods and tinned products for 10p once they reach their best before date.

The waste and recycling advisory body, WRAP, were able to confirm that the Co-op's decision complied with food safety standards.

Figures produced by the Food Standards Agency show that the UK throws away 7.3 million tonnes of food each year.

Source 3 Ways to reduce food waste

What other shops are doing

- **Tesco**: Any waste is either re-used, recycled or turned into energy, and they divert all their waste from landfill. They work with charity Fare Share, who distribute fit-to-eat unsold food to those in need.

- **Waitrose**: Very small amount of food is left over, but they work with Fare Share in the same way as Tesco. 115 branches generate renewable energy from waste.

- **Sainsbury's**: Minimises food waste through accurate forecasting and stock control. Donates to Fare Share, and food that can't be eaten is used to generate electricity through processes such as anaerobic digestion.

The benefits are not just environmental – there are commercial considerations too, as the 'low-waste' message is something that is important to more and more customers. More information can be found at:

- WRAP: household food waste (**www.wrap.org.uk**)
- Love Food Hate Waste campaign (**www.lovefoodhatewaste.com**)
- Fare Share: community food network (**www.fareshare.org.uk**).

Activity 2

Responsible food use

Some supermarkets are already working towards using leftover food to help those in need. Research the policies about not throwing out useable food of other supermarket chains that are not mentioned above.

Activity 3

One personal step

Responsible consumerism needs each individual to make changes. What one personal step could you take to ensure you become a more responsible consumer?

By the end of this lesson you will:
- be able to explain what can make consumerism unethical
- be able to explain the 'social and human cost' of manufacturing in developing countries.

Ethical consumerism means ensuring that the products we buy do not impact negatively on people and the environment. The following are ethical concerns:

- working conditions for staff (including not exploiting child labour)
- fair pay
- environmental sustainability of materials used, for example, recyclable, energy efficient
- animal welfare issues
- ethical profit sharing, for example, Fairtrade
- ethical investment policy, for example, not working with arms dealers.

A major ethical concern is where in the world goods are made and whether anyone has been exploited to make them. Cheap clothing for western markets is often manufactured by multinational companies in developing or newly industrialised countries because:

- wages and other overheads are lower
- capital spending (for example, building a factory) is cheaper
- employment laws are less strict (for example, around children working)
- raw materials are cheaper.

This creates new employment opportunities and income for poor families and export income for the country, but sometimes working conditions are exploitative.

Activity 1

Is low price always fair price?

1. Look at the labels of the shirt/blouse, trousers/skirt, shoes/sandals that you are wearing. Where were they made? Chances are they were made in a developing or newly industrialised country such as China, Sri Lanka, Bangladesh or India.
2. One way to produce low-price goods is to produce them in situations where the workers do not have employment rights and where wages are low (see Source 1). What do you think the five people listed in Source 1 would say in response to this question:

   Do consumers need to pay fairer prices (which sometimes may be more than they pay now) to ensure goods are ethically produced?

Activity 2

What else do you want to know?

Read Source 2, which gives examples of the sorts of questions ethical consumers have asked in the past. What questions would you like to see answered to help you become a more ethical consumer?

The textile, clothing and footwear industry is labour-intensive and factories in developing countries are sometimes associated with the term 'sweatshop', where workers can be treated poorly, with low wages, long hours and poor safety conditions. Fairtrade campaigns have led to codes of conduct and goods being certified, but also to the closure of factories, which can worsen the situation of poor people.

People concerned about clothing production include:

1. Clothing factory worker in a developing country

In some countries farmers have suffered great hardship and been attracted by the possibilities of working in new factories opening up in the towns. It means separation from their families, but often accommodation is provided and regular wages help them assist their family by sending money home. The conditions may not be regulated.

2. Chief Executive Officer (CEO) of a multinational clothing company

Shareholders want improved profits and so manufacturing offshore with cheaper labour and attractive tax deals is an appealing option.

3. Environmentalist

The production and manufacture of textiles, clothing and footwear have high environmental demands, such as water and energy, waste disposal and pollution.

4. Non-Governmental Organisation (NGO) worker

Tight manufacturing deadlines and costs mean unskilled people can be at risk of exploitation. Local NGOs work with vulnerable people to empower them to protect their rights. They also work with governments, businesses and other NGOs to assist in creating better working conditions for factory workers in developing countries.

5. Ethical consumer

Many people feel concerned about the economic, environmental and social problems resulting from some practices in the textile, clothing and footwear manufacturing industry and want to do something about it, such as carefully choosing what they do and don't buy.

Source 1 People concerned about clothing production

You ask … they answer

When it comes to being an ethical consumer it is sometimes difficult to debunk the myth from the reality. Expert advice is often offered to consumers through newspapers and specialist websites. Some common questions and answers are:

Q1: Do some companies only supply green (renewable) energy?

There are very few companies that supply renewable energy alone. One example of these is Bulb, who supply only renewable electricity to homes and businesses.

Q2: Is it more environmentally friendly to buy paper that has been recycled, such as toilet paper and printer paper?

Between 28 and 70 per cent less energy is used to produce recycled paper. It also uses less water. For example, recycled toilet paper uses 50 per cent less energy than creating new toilet paper – this means it is a better option if you want to reduce your carbon impact. The same applies to A4 paper, though the quality isn't as good if you need high-quality printing.

Q3: Which bank is best for ethical policies?

The Co-op Bank was a pioneer for ethical bank accounts and is still the only ethical high street bank, although there are other banks such as Triodos Bank and Norwich & Peterborough Building Society.

Source 2

By the end of this lesson you will:

- be able to explain the different methods used by charities to raise funds
- consider and explain your own view about ethical consumerism and banking.

Over 61 per cent of all adults in the UK donated to charitable causes in 2017. **www.fundraising.co.uk** estimated that the total amount given may be as much as £9.7 billion.

Charities raise funds or supplies through some of the following methods:

- tin shakers, for example, outside supermarkets
- door-to-door collections, for example, envelope returns
- street fundraisers, for example, people who stop you on the street and get you to sign up
- events to raise funds, for example, sponsored runs/coffee mornings
- charity shops, for example, Oxfam/local hospice
- appeals, for example, website donations
- friends of, for example, people who regularly support and give
- public donations of food to food banks
- regular direct debits.

Charities work in many different ways. Two examples are:

- emergency aid – where they help people affected by natural disasters, for example, floods
- development work – where they help people to develop skills to improve their situation.

Food banks

In the UK, more and more people have been turning to food banks as they can't afford to buy the food they need. Food banks are run by a number of organisations throughout the UK including The Trussell Trust. They involve the distribution of a minimum of three days' nutritionally-balanced emergency food, to people who have been referred by care professionals such as health workers, social workers and schools as they are considered to be in crisis. Non-perishable in-date food is donated by the public at a range of places including supermarkets, schools and churches. Over 40 000 volunteers then sort the food into emergency parcels, which are then given to people in need.

Starter

What would you do?

You are walking through the town centre. Someone who you think may be homeless holds out a cup and asks you for some change. What do you do?

Activity 1

What's the priority for your money?

If you decided to donate to charity, would you give for emergency aid or development work? Start by thinking about what each can provide and then decide what your priority would be.

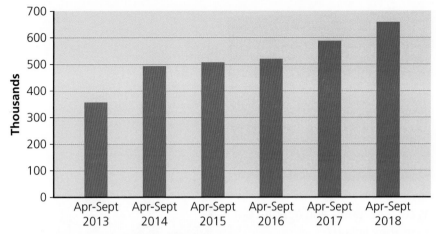

Source 1 The number of three day emergency food parcels given out by the Trussell Trust between April and September in each year from 2013–2018.

There are so many charities trying to raise funds it's not easy to work out which, if any, to give to. If a person does choose to give to charity, it may help them if they consider which charities make the most of their money before they make a final decision. For example:

- What percentage of the donation does the charity use for administration/costs?

- Does the charity maximise the amount it is given by providing 'givers' with a Gift Aid form, which increases the value of the donation? Gift Aid means that you make a tax agreement that allows the charity to claim more money back.

- How they give, for example, if they give via a website such as www.purecharity.com or www.justgiving.com it is important to check whether a percentage of what is given is taken off for administration, as some charity donation websites take a large percentage from the donor before it gets to the charity.

Ethical banking

An ethical bank is one that is concerned with social and environmental issues and also how its investments and loans impact on others.

Other names for such banks are social, alternative, civic or sustainable banks. An ethical bank will make sure their investments reflect their customers' views on issues that are important to them. Many people don't give much thought to how their money will be used by banks and other investment companies. However, some people choose an ethical option for their personal banking.

When surveyed, customers of ethical banks expressed concerns about: animal welfare, child labour, climate change, ecological impact, fair trade, human rights and international development.

Activity 2

Ways to donate

Find out more about ways that people can give to charity.

Activity 3

How would you choose?

What important factors do you think people should consider before investing their money?

Activity 4

Who do I give to?

You've won £1000 to divide equally between one national/local charity and one international charity. Which charities would you choose and why?

By the end of this lesson you will:

- be able to explain how the use of credit cards can lead to a 'debt trap'
- be able to explain how debt can lead to bankruptcy and insolvency
- research and evaluate different types of credit cards that are available
- be able to explain how 'payday loans' can lead to a 'debt trap'.

You will no doubt have heard of terms such as 'debt' and 'credit'. But what do they actually mean and how are they linked?

Most people within the UK will be offered credit and will have debts at some point in their lives. At present the UK personal debt totals are close to £1.6 trillion. Many people's largest debt is their mortgage, which is money they have borrowed to buy a house.

If you manage your debt well by paying back the money at the agreed times, you keep reducing your debt until it is paid off and there are no problems. However, if payments are not kept up then serious consequences can arise such as that in Source 1.

In recent years more and more individuals and businesses have been given credit that they have struggled to pay back. This results in further debt, as additional interest or fines are charged for late repayment. If the debt builds up to a point that the individual or organisation is unable to pay it back they can be declared bankrupt or insolvent. This is likely to have a negative impact on any future credit requests they make.

Source 1 If you are unable to keep up mortgage payments on your home you would either have to sell your home to pay back the debt and move into a cheaper property or rent; or face having your house taken by your mortgage provider and sold to recover the cost.

Starter

Understanding debt and credit

1 In pairs, discuss what you think the terms 'debt' and 'credit' mean. Give examples to show your understanding.
2 Where have you heard these terms? Do you hear them frequently?
3 Do you associate them with being positive or negative?

Activity 1

Why we need credit

1 Make a list of all the different things for which people might be given credit, for example, a mortgage.
2 What problems could arise that would affect a person's ability to pay back their debts?

The number of British businesses collapsing into bankruptcy hit a four-year high recently with one in every 213 companies going into liquidation.

The data was revealed after Carillion, a massive British construction company, collapsed in 2018. It became the UK's biggest corporate failure in a decade and put the construction sector under further strain.

The worst affected sectors were administration and support services, followed by the construction industry and wholesale and retail trade. The three sectors accounted for half of all company insolvencies.

But it wasn't just businesses feeling the strain. Data released by The Insolvency Service also shows that the number of individual people in England and Wales who were declared bankrupt in 2018 increased by 9.4 per cent.

Source 2

Activity 2

The impact of bankruptcy

Source 2 shows the problems that thousands of individuals and businesses are facing. One suggestion to help is for banks to lend more.
1   How would this help?
2   What potential problems might it result in?
3   Do you know any national or local businesses that have closed down? What is likely to be the impact on:
    a   the owners
    b   the employees and their families?

Credit cards

Millions of people in the UK have at least one, if not more, credit or store cards. One of the benefits is that they allow you to purchase something that you can't afford to buy outright at the time you want it. If you pay back the balance on your credit card in full each month you are not charged interest – so, in effect, you have been given interest-free credit to buy the item until the credit card bill is due.

However, if you pay back a small minimum amount of the credit each month, you are charged interest on the outstanding balance. This means that you actually end up paying a lot more for the item than what it would have cost if you bought it outright. This can result in being trapped in a cycle of debt that can be very difficult to get out of.

Many competing credit card companies have seen an opportunity to take advantage of people in the debt trap by offering incentives for them to change company, such as that in Source 4.

You purchase an item for £1000 using your credit or store card.

Your card has an APR (annual percentage rate – interest) of 18%. This is broken down into 12 monthly periods of 1.5% interest charge per month (18 divided by 12 = 1.5% interest per month).

The minimum payment is 2.5% of the total balance; therefore the minimum payment in the first month would be £25 (£1000 divided by 100 x 2.5 = £25).

This means that only £10 of the £25 actually goes to pay back the £1000 used for the purchase. The other £15 goes to pay back the 1.5% interest (2.5% minimum payment (£25) minus 1.5% interest (£15) = £10).

The next month's statement will show the remaining balance as £990 and the next minimum payment will be calculated at £24.75. The payment will cover the £14.85 interest charge and £9.90 of the actual £1000 purchase cost.

The cycle continues until the debt is paid. In this case, assuming that interest rates and other factors stay the same, it would take nearly 13 years (153 months) to pay off the original £1000 debt. £1115.14 would have been paid in interest alone.

Source 3 The credit card minimum payment trap

These types of offers give people an opportunity to pay back more of the amount they owe. However, it can mean that people have (an) additional credit card(s) and therefore may build up debts again.

The government is keen for people to pay back their borrowing more quickly and cheaply and have suggested introducing new rules, including raising the minimum amount that has to be paid each month from around 2–3% to 5%.

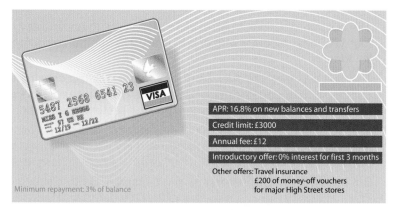

APR: 16.8% on new balances and transfers

Credit limit: £3000

Annual fee: £12

Introductory offer: 0% interest for first 3 months

Other offers: Travel insurance
£200 of money-off vouchers
for major High Street stores

Minimum repayment: 3% of balance

Source 4 Credit card deals can include fees as well as incentives

Activity 3

Which deal is the best?

1 Use the internet to search for different offers that are currently available from credit card companies. Look for details such as those in Source 3 and select one credit card that you think offers the best value. Alternatively, you could use the details in Source 5 for this activity.
2 Imagine you are going on a shopping spree. Make a list of all the different things you would buy and their cost, up to the limit of your chosen card.
3 Now, using the APR and minimum payments rates from the card you have chosen, follow the first four steps in the flow chart in Source 3 to find out:
   a how much the minimum payment would be in the first month
   b how much of that minimum payment is interest, and how much is paying off the original loan.

4 Now work out or estimate the answers to the following questions (use Source 3 to help you). If you only paid the minimum each month:
   a how much would you still owe after twelve months
   b how much would you end up paying to clear your debt, and how much of this is interest
   c how long would it take you to clear the debt
   d how long would it take you to clear the debt if you didn't have to make any interest payments?
5 As a class discuss your findings:
   • Who had the best credit card deal?
   • What problems could people face if they only pay the minimum amount?

Advantages and disadvantages of credit and store cards

• Ease of purchase
• Encourage people to spend money they haven't got
• High interest rates – minimum payment debt trap
• Useful in emergencies
• Incentive offers; e.g. air miles or insurance offers
• Credit card fraud
• Protect your purchases
• Help build a good credit history

Source 5

Activity 4

Pros and cons of credit card use

1 Sort the statements in Source 5 into advantages and disadvantages of using credit or store cards. Add any others you can think of.
2 Plan a social media campaign, series of 'tweets' or radio advert about the do's and don'ts of credit card use and strategies for avoiding debt. Research and include information about where people can seek information should they need advice – The Citizens Advice Bureau is a good starting point.

Payday loans

A relatively new type of loan that you may have seen advertised by various companies on television are 'payday' loans. These are loans that are generally smaller amounts such as £1000, but come with very high interest rates such as 1500 per cent. The loans are meant to tide people over until pay day at which point the loan is paid back. However, while new laws have been implemented to stop unscrupulous companies exploiting people on lower incomes or with bad credit history, many people are still struggling to pay loans back within 31 days, which means they become subject to additional costs.

Payday loan facts and figures

- £260 average loan size
- £100 single most commonly borrowed amount
- 3 in 4 customers take out more than one loan per year
- 6 loans is the average customers take out in a year
- 25–30 year olds are the age group most likely to take out the loans
- single people are more likely to take out loans than couples
- renters of housing rather than owners are more likely to have loans
- households that earn less than £1500 per month are more likely to take out a payday loan.

Source 6

Danny's story

When a 19-year-old university student took out a payday loan 10 years ago for £100, he had little idea how much it would actually cost him to repay.

The original deal saw him repaying £128 after 22 days, which seemed reasonable to him. And as soon as he had settled his debt, the loan company then offered him another loan of £420 which he could pay back in 38 days. He agreed but was shocked to find that he now owed £585 when he came to repay the loan.

Unable to afford this, the young man obtained another loan, from another high-cost short-term lender, for £275. When the interest was charged, this debt quickly grew to £538.

During the next 10 years, the borrower bounced between payday lenders and borrowed hundreds of pounds at a time to pay off the different companies who were all chasing him.

Incredibly, even though he had so much debt, he was still able to obtain loans which were paid straight into his account within minutes of texts being sent and received.

To date, he believes he has paid almost £19,000 in interest to payday lenders.

Source 7

Activity 5

Temptation

Do you think credit cards and payday loans provide too much 'temptation' for people? Discuss your view with a partner and then as a class.

By the end of this lesson you will:

- be able to explain the emotional and financial costs of misusing money
- research and evaluate solutions to financial problems.

Starter

Money, money, money

Everyone needs money in some shape or form. Using money can be a positive experience but misusing money has risks attached. Look at Source 1. Of all these different ways that a teenager might use money, which one might cause the biggest problems and why?

Teenagers and money

The key financial concerns/experiences of pupils between the ages of 11 and 16 include:

- saving money
- managing pocket and gifted money
- mobile phone bills and tariffs
- which bank account to choose
- debit cards
- use of electronic banking
- earnings from part-time employment
- getting around, for example, bus or train
- buying clothing and other goods
- buying gifts for others
- selling goods.

Source 1

Part of becoming an independent adult is learning how to manage money. This starts with the situations that teenagers might face in Source 1, but money worries usually increase as we get older. On pages 148–150 are three case studies that describe typical problems that adults face in managing their finances.

Activity 1

The cost of money

Read the three case studies on pages 149–151 and answer the questions that follow them.

Case study

1: Sheila, Sam and Kirsty

Sheila is a single parent who lives with Sam, 15 and Kirsty, 13. She is a generous mum who enjoys buying gifts for her children and indeed for herself. She rents her home and doesn't manage to save anything – there is no money left at the end of each month. A lot of the time Sheila lives on her **credit cards** – she never manages to pay off more than the minimum monthly requirement. The children aren't aware of this and are used to having whatever they ask for.

Cutbacks at Sheila's place of work mean that many staff are faced with the possibility of **redundancy**. Sheila has only been with the company for four years so if she loses her job she won't get a big redundancy pay-out.

On the same day that she hears that 50 per cent of employees may need to be made redundant, she also receives her latest credit card statements. She owes about £5500 in total to three different credit card companies. She knows she is going to have to change her spending habits. What is worrying her even more is how to break this news to Sam and Kirsty. She knows they won't be happy about how this will affect them but what can she do?

Questions

a What kind of things might Sheila have bought using credit cards?

b Sheila feels that she has lost control – why is this the case?

c How do you think Sam and Kirsty will react to the news their mother is going to give them? What will they be most worried about?

d Sheila decides she must talk about 'needs versus wants' with Sam and Kirsty. What does this mean?

e What could each member of the family do to improve the situation?

Case study

2: Rafik

Rafik is 22 and is now living back at home with his parents after completing his university degree. He is not yet earning enough to have to start paying back his **student loan** from university days. He has a job assisting a local charity. It is not well paid, but he enjoys it.

Rafik has a lively social life with all his cousins and a great group of friends. They enjoy socialising and he enjoys looking good and keeping up with fashionable

→

trends – clothes, phones, music, etc. In addition to his university fees, Rafik has run up **debts** of almost £7000, mainly with several **store cards**, and he is only able to make the minimum payments on these. The store cards charge a high rate of interest and his debt is building every month. It had seemed so easy to get **credit** at the time – all you had to do was fill in a form and you didn't have to pay for it all straight away. Some of the shops even offered a massive discount on the day you signed up to their card. He hadn't realised that the interest rate (called the **APR** or Annual Percentage Rate) was much higher than the bank would have charged on an **overdraft**. Rafik now owes much more than he originally spent.

Rafik saw a documentary about people and debt on TV. He decided to contact a **money adviser** (a free service). He could then work out how to pay off his debts, although he knew it would take a long time. After talking his problems through, he has learned how to budget and has taken on a second job so that he can clear his store card debts more quickly and start to think about how he will pay off his student loan.

Questions

a What kind of shops offer store cards?

b How big a factor in building up his debt was the need to keep up with others?

c How might huge debts impact on Rafik's emotional health?

d What suggestions for improving his situation would Rafik have received when he used the free financial advice service?

e How does someone judge between what is promoted as a 'good deal' and what they can really afford? What pros and cons do they have to consider?

Source 2 Lottery win Bus driver Kevin Halstead drove the 125 bus on the same route from Bolton to Preston for 17 years before winning £2.3 million on the lottery. In this photo he and his partner Josephine Jones celebrate their win. When he won he said he wouldn't quit his job because he would miss his colleagues. It seems money can't buy you friends, or happiness.

Activity 2

Money can't buy you happiness

Look at Source 2. What costs nothing and brings *you* happiness?

Case study

3: Summer

Summer is 32 and single. She has a mortgage on her duplex apartment in a nice part of town. She works as a dental nurse and after monthly deductions (income tax, national insurance and pension contribution) her take home pay is £1650. The dental practice used to be very busy and she earned even more through working later in the evenings and over the occasional weekend. However, although Summer earns less money now, she has kept to her previous lifestyle. She has done this by using credit cards and now owes £17,000 spread over many different cards. She likes to eat out with friends, Friday night is 'girls' night out' and she always has the latest mobile phone and takes whatever contract she is offered in the shop.

With the situation at work not improving Summer realised she couldn't afford to carry on living at

that rate. After seeing an advert on television she decided to take out a **secured consolidation loan** of £18,000. This paid off all her credit cards and put all her debts into one place. However, in order to secure the loan she had to tie it to her apartment as a guarantee.

To keep the monthly payments as low as possible, she took out the loan over 20 years at a monthly repayment of £150. However, Summer continued to spend as though nothing had changed and missed some payments on her loan. She took out a few new store cards to cheer herself up.

Summer hadn't looked at the small print of the loan and didn't realise that because she'd borrowed over 20 years at an APR of about eight per cent, over the total time of the loan she would actually have to pay back over £35,000. With that and her new store cards, she built up a total debt of over £45,000 as well as having to pay her mortgage. She could not afford to keep up her payments and **defaulted on her mortgage**.

By the time Summer sought professional money advice it was too late and she was advised to go bankrupt. She lost her apartment – it was **repossessed** – and she had to start again, only this time she won't be able to get a mortgage or a loan, or use credit or store cards for the next year.

Questions

a Summer saw an advert offering to consolidate all her loans into one. She thought it seemed too good to be true. Was it?

b Spending to cheer yourself up (retail therapy) is not unusual. In Summer's case it cost more than she had bargained for. How might spending beyond her means affect her emotions and relationships with others?

c Summer responded to a TV advert offering what looked like a good loan. Why might shopping around for the most appropriate financial products and services be a more sensible solution?

d If you don't understand the financial implications of living independently (without parental support) where would you go for help and advice?

By the end of this lesson you will:

- be able to explain different types of business structure and how they can be organised
- evaluate and explain the advantages and disadvantages of tall and flat business structures
- be able to explain how businesses are structured and organised depending on the product/service they provide
- produce a chart showing the structure and organisation of your school.

Starter

What makes a successful product?

1 Make a list of the latest gadgets you have bought recently or would like to buy.
2 Choose one from your list and give reasons why you think it has become so successful.
3 Speak to two other people in your class to find out what product they chose and the reasons why they think their product became successful. Were their reasons for the product's success the same as yours?

Businesses come in all shapes and sizes, offering a wide range of products and services. There are four main types of business:

- **Sole traders** – businesses owned by one person, although they may employ others. A plasterer is an example of this as they provide a service and are often self-employed.

- **Partnerships** – businesses that are owned by two people or more.

- **Limited companies** – companies that have their own legal identity and are split into equal parts – called shares – which are available to buy. There are two types of Limited companies – 'private' and 'public'.

- **Franchise** – when a person buys into an existing company and has the right to use an existing idea or product, for example, Subway is a franchise.

The overall aim of a business is to make more money than it spends. This is known as 'profit'.

Some of the reasons for success you may have come up with in the Starter Activity are: the use of new technology; successful marketing; low costs; or solves a significant problem. You may or may not have thought about how the businesses that produce the products are organised. But the organisation and structure of any business is just as essential for success as the idea, product or service it offers.

Business structures

Most businesses are structured in one of two main ways, usually depending on their size. Both have their advantages and disadvantages (see below). Other types of business structure include **centralised**, **collaborative** and **matrix**.

1 Tall (hierarchical)

In a tall organisation, employees are ranked at different levels, each one above another. At each level, except the bottom, one person has a team of people reporting to them.

Source 1 The tall structure

Advantages	Disadvantages
Each manager has a small number of employees under their control. This means that employees can be closely supervised.	The freedom and responsibility of employees is restricted.
There is a clear management structure.	Decision-making could be slowed down as approval may be needed by each of the layers of authority.
The function of each layer will be clear and distinct. There will be clear lines of responsibility and control.	Communication has to take place through many layers of management.
There is a clear progression and promotion ladder.	There are high management costs because managers are generally paid more than subordinates. Each layer will tend to pay its managers more money than the layer below it.

Source 2 Advantages and disadvantages of the tall structure

2 Flat

In a flat hierarchy, the chain of command is much shorter (fewer layers) and the span of control wider.

Source 3 The flat structure

Advantages	Disadvantages
More/greater communication between management and workers.	Workers may have more than one manager/boss.
Better team spirit.	May limit/hinder the growth of the organisation.
Less bureaucracy and easier decision-making.	Structure usually limited to small organisations.
Fewer levels of management, which includes benefits such as lower costs, as managers are generally paid more.	Function of each department/person could be blurred and merge into the job roles of others.

Source 4 Advantages and disadvantages of the flat structure

Activity 1

Which is the right type of business structure?

Using the information from Sources 1–4, produce two spidergrams showing the advantages and disadvantages of the two main types of business structure.

Activity 2

Research a company business structure

1   Choose one of the well-known companies below. Use the internet to research the type of business structure it uses. Before you carry out your research, try and predict the type of business structure you would expect the company to use based on what you know about the company already. Were you right?

NIKE   BP   TESCO   VODAFONE   TOYOTA   McDONALD'S

2   Discuss your findings as a class:
   a   Is there one business structure that is more common than the others?
   b   If so, why do you think this is?
   c   Why do you think an appropriate business structure is so important?

Activity 3

What about your school?

What type of business structure does your school use and why?

Business organisations

Each business will organise its structure to increase its efficiency and productivity. Different types of organisation can be seen in Sources 5–8.

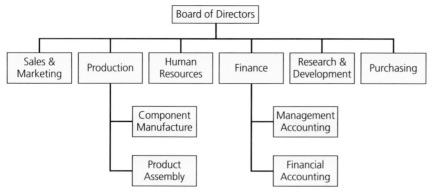

Source 5 Organisation by function

```
                    ┌──────────────────┐
                    │ Board of Directors│
                    └──────────────────┘
```

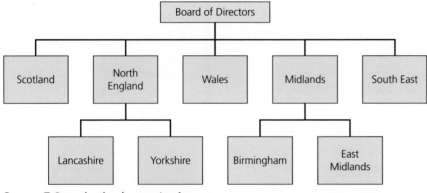

Source 6 Organisation by product

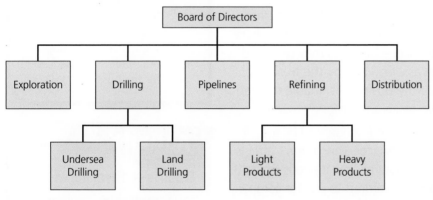

Source 7 Organisation by area/region

Source 8 Organisation by process

Activity 4

Organising a school

Although your school isn't a profit-making business, it does provide a service. Using the information about business structures and organisations, produce a business structure for your school. You would obviously start with the head teacher at the top. Before you begin, you may wish to work with a partner to make a list of the different roles you know that staff do in your school, for example, deputy heads, assistant heads, heads of year, department heads and so on.

Activity 5

Pitch a product

Imagine you are going on *Dragons' Den*. In pairs, think of a product you would want to get funding for. Pitch your product to your partner, explaining the type of business structure you would employ and how you would organise it.

Activity 6

Structuring your own business

Which type of business structure would you feel most comfortable leading and why? Discuss your answer with others in the group.

Activity 7

Think about similar business structures

Can you think of other examples in which structures, similar to those you have discussed about in businesses and your school, are needed? Make a list of your ideas.

By the end of this lesson you will:
- be able to explain the different types of finance available to business and choose which are most appropriate for different situations
- be able to explain the importance of businesses in our society.

Starter

Reasons businesses need finance

In pairs, make a list of all the reasons you can think of why new businesses need finance.

One of the most important factors in business is profit. However, before any business can make a profit, it needs finance to start up – maybe to buy equipment or help with the day-to-day running of the company. Sometimes finance will be needed for a short period of time – maybe to overcome a shortage of funds; for example, if a customer hasn't paid on time – while on other occasions it may be needed for much longer; for example, if a new building or large machinery is being purchased.

Business finance

There are two main types of finance available to businesses. These are **internal** and **external** finance.

Internal finances are those that come from within the business itself. There is no cost to the business as such, but by funding one particular aspect of a business it could mean that you no longer have enough to fund something else. This is known as the **opportunity cost**. An example would be if you have used funding to purchase new premises, which could mean that you can't afford to buy new equipment.

External finances usually involve borrowing money and paying back an additional amount in the form of **interest**, or giving away a share in the business. To secure external finance, a business may be asked to provide **security** in the form of an asset owned by the business; for example, property or machinery. If the business is unable to keep up payments, the asset can be sold to reclaim the money owed.

The type of external finance a business chooses is influenced by the amount it needs to borrow and what it needs it for. This, in turn, affects how long it needs the loan for and the amount of time it needs to pay it back; for example, you wouldn't choose an overdraft to pay for company cars as you would want to lease these over a longer period of time.

Source 1 shows examples of the types of external finance available.

Activity 1

Why businesses need finance

1   Choose a particular type of business of interest to you, and number each reason for finance in your starter activity list in order of importance for your choice.
2   Discuss:
- Was it difficult to number your reasons in order of importance?
- If so, what does this suggest about the difficulties businesses have when starting up or allocating finance?
- Were there any reasons that had to be financed for the business to work?

Activity 2

Business financing

1   In small groups, choose one or two of the different types of business finance in Source 1 (look up any terms you don't understand). Use the internet to research:
   a   how the finance is given
   b   examples of this type of finance.
   Feed back the information you have found to the class.

Short term (usually up to 12 months)	Medium term (usually 1–3 years)	Long term (usually more than 3 years)
overdraft from bank	**bank loan**	bank loan
factoring	**hire purchase/lease**	**mortgage**
trade/store credit.	**grant.**	hire purchase/lease
		venture capital/new investor

Source 1 The finance timeline

Activity 3

The most appropriate finance

A business uses finance for a variety of reasons. Make a copy of the table below. Using the information in Source 2, decide which type of finance is most appropriate for each. Add any other examples you can think of.

Overdraft/ credit	Bank loan	Hire purchase/ lease	Mortgage	Company profits	Investor

Reasons for finance

a   Temporary shortage of funds
b   Equipment
c   Marketing
d   Company cars, lorries, etc.
e   Computers
f   Buying property/premises
g   Start-up costs
h   New premises (not owned by the business)
i   'Buying' goods before paying for them
j   New staff
k   Staff training
l   Research and development

Source 2

Activity 4

Give advice

Read each of the scenarios in Source 3. For each one give advice as to what type of finance is most appropriate and why. You may need to advise using more than one source of finance.

a   A brand new business wishes to stream video games, movies and music over the internet and needs money for the appropriate computer technology, servers, licences, app development and advertising.

b   A small independent gardening business (one person) wishes to buy a second-hand van and employ a new member of staff.

Activity 5

The importance of business

Why are businesses, whatever their size, so important to our society? What problems would we have if businesses couldn't get finance when they needed it?

c   A well-established florist wants to expand their business by relocating to bigger premises on the main shopping street in their town centre. They also want to expand their product to include balloons, chocolates and other goods that can be delivered with their flowers.

Source 3 Finance scenarios

157

By the end of this lesson you will:

- understand what it means to be enterprising and give examples of successful entrepreneurs
- identify potential risks within business and how to manage them
- be able to explain the qualities needed to be a successful entrepreneur.

Starter

Making life easier

Think about a typical school day, from waking up in the morning to when you go to bed. Now make a list of all the things you have that make your life easier or more comfortable; for example, hot running water, cold milk from the fridge, television, alarm clock, car, bike and so on.

Consider for a moment how different your life would be if you didn't have these things, for example, no hot running water because boilers weren't invented. Everything you use every day has been made and when something is made there is an opportunity to make money from it.

You will no doubt have heard of names such as Deborah Meaden, Alan Sugar and Karen Brady. Each of them has become very famous and also very rich. They are what are known as 'entrepreneurs'. An entrepreneur is an individual who takes calculated financial risks to launch a new financial venture or business.

Activity 1

What makes an entrepreneur?

Make a list of any entrepreneurs you may have heard of. It may help to think of a product or service and then who created it, for example, the Dyson vacuum cleaner was created by Sir James Dyson.

Case study

Peter Jones

Today, Peter Jones' net worth is estimated at over £485 million. But he hasn't always enjoyed such riches...

Educated at both private and state schools, Peter began his career aged just 16 when he founded a tennis academy. He then went on to set up a computer business, followed by a computer support company. A less successful investment in the restaurant trade led to the loss of his house, cars and computer business, after which he joined the giant company Siemens Nixdorf and ran its computer business in the UK. In 1998 he founded a telecommunications firm (Phones International Group) that now generates revenues in excess of £200 million per year.

It was the TV series *Dragons' Den* which first saw Peter Jones become a household name in 2005. He has invested over £4,085,667 while working on the show and some of his more successful gambles include Levi Roots' Reggae Reggae Sauce, Love da Popcorn, Rempods and Bare Naked Foods.

Apart from *Dragons' Den*, Peter has also worked on two other major television projects.

- *American Inventor*, on which Peter Jones was a judge, became a number one hit in the USA. He sold it to the American Broadcasting Company (ABC).

- *Tycoon*, the programme where Peter searches for entrepreneurs with ideas that he can turn into profitable companies, achieved viewing figures in excess of 2.1 million people.

Peter Jones has many interests across a broad range of businesses, including publishing, TV, entertainment, food, new media and product design which employ over 1000 people, generating sales upwards of $370 million.

In 2009 Peter Jones founded the National Enterprise Academy (NEA). It is a centre of excellence for enterprise and entrepreneurship and has three campuses in the UK. Peter was awarded a CBE in the 2009 New Year Honours List for services to business, entrepreneurship and young people.

Peter Jones also gives a lot back to society. In 2005 he established The Peter Jones Foundation to offer funding and support to underprivileged children in the UK. He is also keen to support entrepreneurial talent in the UK, helping young people and young enterprises to flourish.

Source 1

Activity 2

Research an entrepreneur

1 Select one of the entrepreneurs from your Starter activity list and use the internet to research them in greater detail. Produce a case study similar to the one about Peter Jones in Source 1. Try to find out the following details:
   - when they were born and other personal details
   - their first invention/idea
   - how they got their idea 'up and running'
   - when they made their first million
   - any setbacks they had
   - what they have done since.
2 In small groups, talk about what you found out about your entrepreneur.
   - What do they all have in common?
   - Did they all face the same problems?
   - What do they tell you about being successful?

One of the qualities that all the people you have researched will have in common is that they are 'enterprising'. You will have probably come across this word before, and maybe even taken part in enterprise days or events such as *Dragons' Den* or *The Apprentice* style competitions. But what qualities do you need to be enterprising? Source 2 (see page 165) shows some of these. A simple way to remember these qualities are PIER: Persuasion, Idea, Energy, Risk.

If you have all these qualities then setting up a successful business is more likely, but will still require a great deal of hard work and commitment. However, if you are lacking any of the qualities then success is very difficult to achieve.

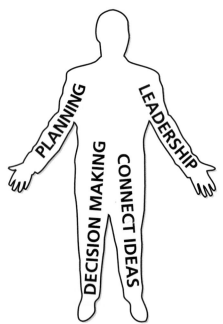

Persuasion: you will need to persuade other people to lend you money and join your venture (P)

Idea: you will need an initial idea, product or service; maybe one that no one else has thought of (I)

Full of energy: you must keep the business going even when faced with competition (E)

Be able to take calculated risks: all businesses take risks to some extent, particularly those that are successful (R)

Source 2 Enterprising qualities

SWOT

One way to help manage risks associated with a new enterprise venture is to carry out what is called a SWOT analysis. A SWOT analysis is a strategic method that is used to evaluate the **strengths** (S), **weaknesses** (W), **opportunities** (O) and **threats** (T) of any new business ideas.

Strengths: things that the business is in control of that give it an advantage over others.	Weaknesses: things that the business is in control of that place the business at a disadvantage compared to others.
Opportunities: other chances outside the control of the business to make greater sales or profits if our initial business is successful.	Threats: problems outside the control of the business that could put the business at risk, such as other businesses offering the same product or service.

Source 3

Activity 3

Enterprise qualities

1 For each enterprise quality in Source 2, explain the problems an entrepreneur would face if they didn't have that quality.
2 Rank the qualities in order from the most important to the least and explain your order. Is this possible to do?
3 Why is financial risk such an important issue and a reason why many people are put off? For example, think about what could be lost if the business venture failed.
4 Do you think you have the qualities to be an entrepreneur?
5 Do you think others think you have the qualities to be an entrepreneur?

Activity 4

Carry out a SWOT

1 Read Source 3. In pairs or small groups, carry out a SWOT analysis on the latest Apple iPhone. Use the internet to research it further if you need more specific detail.
2 Work in pairs to make a list of ways in which you can minimise the threats and maximise the opportunities for the latest Apple iPhone.

You probably identified that one of the strengths of the iPhone is the Apple brand name. Developing a strong brand name that customers trust is important if a business is to become a success.

Case study:

Apple iPhone X

Apple is an American company that has gone from strength to strength, with much hype surrounding the new products they release. In 2018 they released the iPhone X, which was considered by many reviews to be a 'huge leap forward' after concerns that recent versions of the iPhone had been too similar.

The iPhone X offered a range of new and improved features that some critics said made it the 'nearest to perfect phone on the market'. The features include: wireless charging; removal of the 'home' button and introduction of 'gestures' to control the phone; an all glass body, giving it a higher quality look; facial recognition which replaced the existing touch ID and unlocks the phone quicker; an A11 processor which makes the phone faster and better than ever before in terms of its capabilities; water resistance to a depth of 1.5 metres for up to 30 minutes. A novel addition was the 'animoji' feature which uses the facial recognition to identify expressions via the iPhone X camera, to animate various 3D animated emojis that can be sent as a video file with sound.

However, there were also a number of features that were removed or changed from previous versions of the iPhones which many reviews were critical of: initially the iPhone X was only available in Space Gray or Silver; Touch ID and iris sensors were removed so the phone could no longer be unlocked with fingerprints or the eye; there was no 3.5 mm audio headphone jack which meant buying an additional connector to connect existing headphones; the battery cannot be removed and updated; unlike Android phones there was no 'split tasking' meaning that you can only run one app at a time. Arguably the most talked about issue surrounding the iPhone X was the price tag, which was around the £1000 at launch. A report in January 2019 stated that due to slow sales in some parts of the world, Apple are planning to reduce the price of the iPhone X by fifteen per cent to try and increase sales.

In 2018, reports from data analyst companies Strategy Research and Counterpoint Research, stated that smartphone sales stopped growing for the first time ever in history. Phone companies still managed to shift 376 million devices in the last three months of 2018, however over the course of the whole year there was a five per cent drop in sales when compared to 2017. Apple and Samsung both sold fewer phones, while Huawei and Xiaomi both sold more.

Will saturation of the mobile phone market continue to affect Apple in the future? What do they need to do to increase their sales and stave off competition from other brands?

Activity 5

A world without risk

What would the world be like if we didn't have entrepreneurs who are prepared to be enterprising and take positive risks?

Index

Text and photo credits

Text credits

p.10 Article by © Debbie Godfrey, 'Parenting – the most natural thing in the world?'; **p.12–3** From Childline https://www.childline.org.uk/info-advice/bullying-abuse-safety/abuse-safety/sexual-abuse/ © NSPCC; **p.20** Adapted from www.healthforteens.co.uk; **p.31** Results from the National Survey of Sexual Attitudes and Lifestyles (Natsal). © 2019 Natsal; **p.32** Research Highlights for Children's Online Safety #114 June 2017, The Impact of Online Pornography on Children and Young People, from the UK Council for Child Internet Safety (UKCCIS) © Crown copyright; **p.33** 'The Dark Reason Porn Stars Keep Dying' by Neelam Tailor, 13 Jan 2018, UNILAD. © 2018 The LADbible Group Ltd; **p.39** Tackling 'cuckooing' and county lines drug networks, Crimestoppers Trust, 2019; **p.40** www.gov.uk/government/publications/communicating-the-uk-chief-medicalofficers- alcohol-guidelines; **p.47** 'Government accused of cutting vital drug and alcohol services as £43m slashed from addiction budgets' by Lizzy Buchan, 25 September 2017, ©The Independent, https://www.independent.co.uk/news/uk/politics/government–cuts–drug–alcohol–services–43m–addiction–budgets–jonathan–ashworth–nhs–a7964826.html; **p.51** From Mind, www.mind.org.uk/information-support/types-of-mental-health-problems/ **p.55** 'Snapchat dysmorphia: Teenagers are getting plastic surgery to look like selfie filters' by Chelsea Ritschel, 6 August 2018, © The Independent https://www.independent.co.uk/life–style/plastic–surgery–cosmetic–snapchat–teenagers–millennials–dysmorphia–bdd–a8474881.html; **p.67** NHS Digital, Statistics on Obesity, Physical Activity and Diet, England, 2019, https://digital.nhs.uk/data-and-information/publications/statistical/statistics-on-obesity-physical-activity-and-diet/statistics-on-obesity-physical-activity-and-diet-england-2019/part-4-childhood-obesity; **p.79** Extract from 'I'm A Celeb's Jack Maynard issues apology for deleted 2011 tweet about rape', https://www.radiotimes.com/news/tv/2017–11–29/jack–maynard–twitter–im–a–celebrity/. Used with permission from Radio Times; **p.80** 'Man jailed for four months over Facebook threat to kill MP', 12 April 2017, Press Association, © Guardian, News & Media Limited. Used with permission from PA Media; **p.81** From 'Bullying and cyberbullying: Advice for parents and carers to help keep children safe from bullying, wherever it happens', © 2019 NSPCC. https://www.nspcc.org.uk/what–is–child–abuse/types–of–abuse/bullying–and–cyberbullying/; **p.84** 'What is a gang?' © 2019 Bedfordshire Police; **p.105** 'What Do We Do with a Variation?' from *When I Dance* by James Berry, Hamish Hamilton, 1988. Reproduced with permission of Bloodaxe Books; **pp.106–7** Data from Eurostat https://ec.europa.eu/eurostat/statistics-explained/index.php/Asylum_quarterly_report; **p.108** 'As ending HIV transmissions in the UK becomes a reality, we must support those living with the virus to thrive, and end the stigma they face', 1 December 2018, https://www.tht.org.uk/news/ending-hiv-transmissions-uk-becomes-reality-we-must-support-those-living-virus-thrive. Used with permission from Terrence Higgins Trust; **p.113** data from the Democracy Index © The Economist Intelligence Unit Limited 2018; **p.114** Data from a survey of 13,000 children aged 7 to 11 backed by University College London in 2018, reported on 19 January 2018 at https://www.prima.co.uk/family/kids/news/a42250/primary–school–children–career–aspirations–drawing–the–future–report/#sidepanel; **p.115** 'Reality check: life behind Insta–glam image of 'influencers' by Suzanne Bearne, 17 Mar, 2019, © Guardian News & Media Limited. https://www.theguardian.com/money/2019/mar/17/instagram–social–media–influencers–reality. Used with permission from Guardian News & Media Limited.

Photo credits

p.2 © Rawpixel.com - stock.adobe.com; **p.4** *tl* © Elenathewise – Fotolia; *tc* © Future Digital Design – Fotolia.com; *tr* © Yuri Arcurs – Fotolia; *bl* © Rawpixel.com - stock.adobe.com; *bc* © Rob – Fotolia; *br* © Monkey Business - stock.adobe.com; **p.6** *t* © biker3 – stock.adobe.com; *b* © Africa Studio – stock.adobe.com; **p.8** *tl* © Shutterstock / Vasyl Shulga; *tr* © brain2hands - stock.adobe.com; *bl* © Mariusz Blach – Fotolia; *br* © Caroline Sylger Jones / Alamy; **p.14** © se media - stock.adobe.com; **p.16** Reproduced by kind permission of The Survivors Trust; **p.17** *b* Reproduced by kind permission of Women's Aid; **p.18** © Monkey Business - stock.adobe.com; **p.19** © SBphotos - stock.adobe.com; **p.24** © Prostock-studio - stock.adobe.com; **p.34** © Antonioguillem - stock.adobe.com; **p.36** © Granger/Shutterstock; **pp.38–9** © lukaspuchrik - stock.adobe.com; **p.39** Reproduced by kind permission of Crimestoppers Trust; **p.41** Picture copyright https://drinkaware.co.uk/; **p.48** *t* © fizkes - stock.adobe.com; *c* © Leonid - stock.adobe.com; *b* © LIGHTFIELD STUDIOS - stock.adobe.com; **p.52** © pathdoc - stock.adobe.com; **p.53** ©Кирилл Рыжов - stock.adobe.com; **p.55** © blackday - stock.adobe.com; **p.56** © Syda Productions - stock.adobe com; **p.62** *l* © Stuart Black / Alamy Stock Photo; *c* © Amy Cicconi / Alamy Stock Photo; *r* © Bosse Haglund / Alamy; **p.64** Public Health England. Antibiotic Guardian Leaflet https://antibioticguardian.com/; **p.65** *t* Public Health England; *b* Public Health England; **p.70** © Shutterstock / Rob Wilson; **p.73** Public Health England; **p.75** © Gorodenkoff - stock.adobe.com; **p.76** © Sean Gladwell – Fotolia; **p.77** © luismolinero - stock.adobe.com; **p.78** © drserg /123RF.com; **p.91** *t* © claireliz – Fotolia; *second* © S. Mohr Photography – Fotolia; *third* © Shutterstock / Lolostock; *fourth* © SunnyS - stock.adobe.com; *fifth* © Stockbyte/Photolibrary Group Ltd; *b* © Couperfield – Fotolia; **p.98** *t* © zirconicusso - stock.adobe.com; *b* © Matt Cardy/Getty Images; **p.106** *t* © Craig Stennett / Alamy Stock Photo; *b* © Tim Ockenden/PA Archive/PA Images; **p.109** © GARY DOAK / Alamy Stock Photo; **p.112** *t* © ZUMA Press, Inc. / Alamy Stock Photo; *b* © Mieszko9 - stock.adobe.com; **p.122** © Crown copyright, Open Government Licence; **p.128** © Amazon; **p.134** © Brian Jackson - stock.adobe.com; **p.138** © Andrey Popov - stock.adobe.com; **p.144** © ibreakstock - stock.adobe.com; **p.147** © Rawpixel.com - stock.adobe.com; **p.149** *t* © brankatekic – Fotolia; *b* © Yves Damin - stock.adobe.com; **p.150** © Dave Thompson/PA Archive/PA Images; **p.151** © Olivier – Fotolia; **p.157** *t* © weedezign - stock.adobe.com; *c* © Giovanni Cardillo - stock.adobe.com; *b* © Monkey Business - Fotolia.com; **p.159** © JEP Celebrity Photos / Alamy Stock Photo.

l = left, *r* = right, *c* = centre, *t* = top, *b* = bottom